# ARMAGEDDON & SON

Oni Press

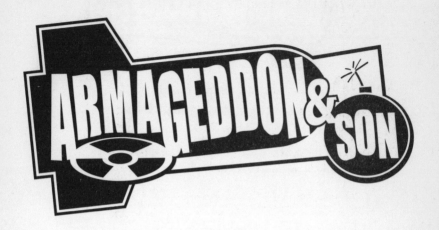

Edited by **RANDAL C. JARRELL**
Production assistance by **KEITH WOOD**

Published by Oni Press, Inc.
**JOE NOZEMACK**, publisher • **JAMES LUCAS JONES**, editor in chief
**RANDAL C. JARRELL**, managing editor • **MARYANNE SNELL**, director of marketing and sales

ONI PRESS, INC.
1305 SE MLK Blvd.
Suite A
Portland, OR 97202
USA

www.onipress.com

First edition: October 2005
ISBN 1-932664-33-5

1 3 5 7 9 10 8 6 4 2
PRINTED IN CANADA.

# JOHN LAYMAN
writer • letterer • creator

# DAVE DUMEER
artist • co-creator

For my Dad, obviously.

—JL

This book is for Linda.
Thanks, Mom.

—David

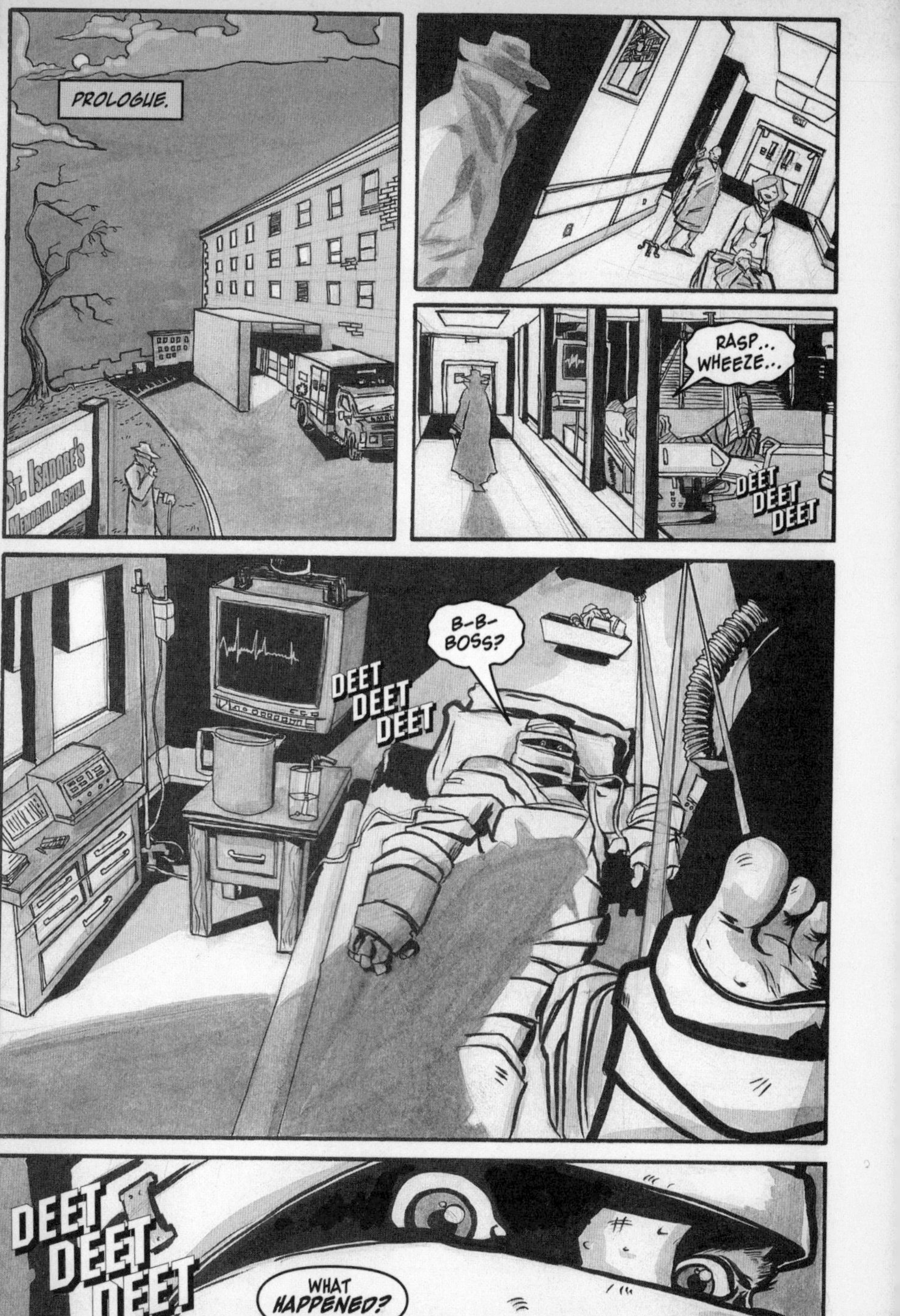
PROLOGUE.
ST. ISADORE'S MEMORIAL HOSPITAL
RASP... WHEEZE...
DEET DEET DEET
B-B-BOSS?
DEET DEET DEET
DEET DEET DEET
WHAT HAPPENED?

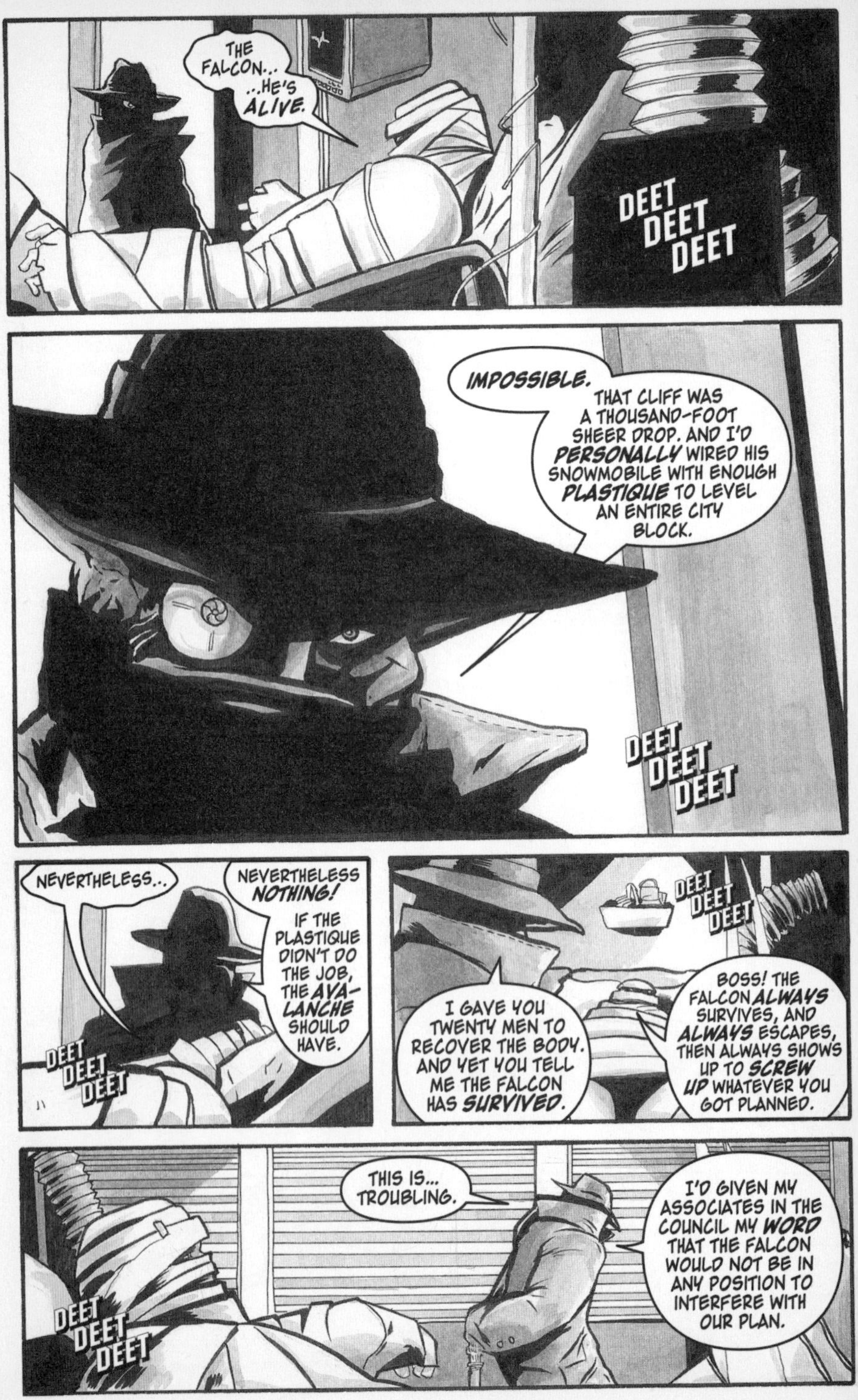
THE FALCON... ...HE'S ALIVE.
DEET DEET DEET
IMPOSSIBLE.
THAT CLIFF WAS A THOUSAND-FOOT SHEER DROP. AND I'D PERSONALLY WIRED HIS SNOWMOBILE WITH ENOUGH PLASTIQUE TO LEVEL AN ENTIRE CITY BLOCK.
DEET DEET DEET
NEVERTHELESS...
NEVERTHELESS NOTHING!
IF THE PLASTIQUE DIDN'T DO THE JOB, THE AVA-LANCHE SHOULD HAVE.
DEET DEET DEET
DEET DEET DEET
I GAVE YOU TWENTY MEN TO RECOVER THE BODY. AND YET YOU TELL ME THE FALCON HAS SURVIVED.
BOSS! THE FALCON ALWAYS SURVIVES, AND ALWAYS ESCAPES, THEN ALWAYS SHOWS UP TO SCREW UP WHATEVER YOU GOT PLANNED.
THIS IS... TROUBLING.
I'D GIVEN MY ASSOCIATES IN THE COUNCIL MY WORD THAT THE FALCON WOULD NOT BE IN ANY POSITION TO INTERFERE WITH OUR PLAN.
DEET DEET DEET

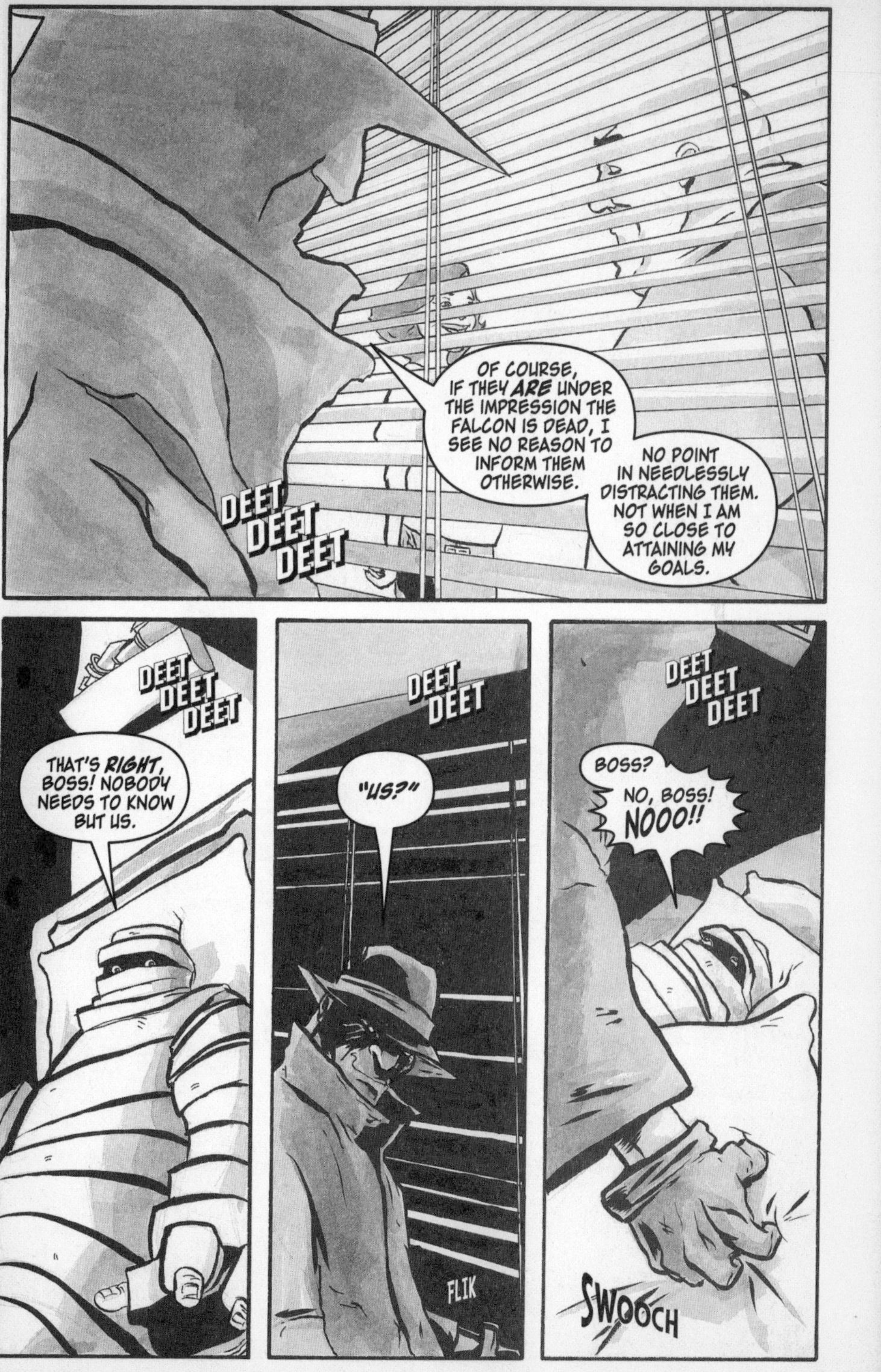
OF COURSE, IF THEY ARE UNDER THE IMPRESSION THE FALCON IS DEAD, I SEE NO REASON TO INFORM THEM OTHERWISE.
NO POINT IN NEEDLESSLY DISTRACTING THEM. NOT WHEN I AM SO CLOSE TO ATTAINING MY GOALS.
DEET DEET DEET
DEET DEET DEET
THAT'S RIGHT, BOSS! NOBODY NEEDS TO KNOW BUT US.
DEET DEET
"US?"
FLIK
DEET DEET DEET
BOSS?
NO, BOSS! NOOO!!
SWOOCH

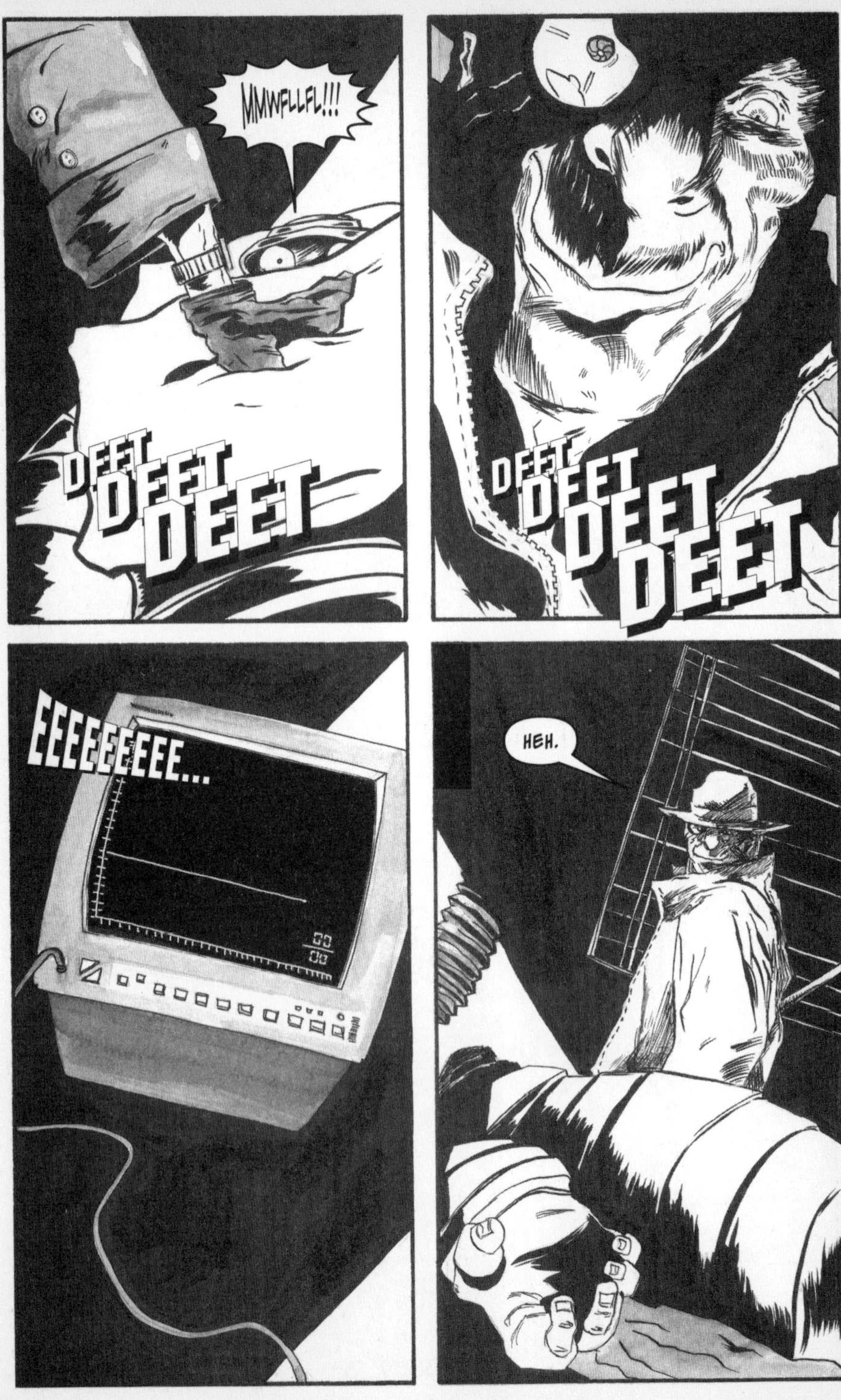
MMWFLLFL!!!
DEET DEET DEET
DEET DEET DEET DEET
EEEEEEEEE...
HEH.

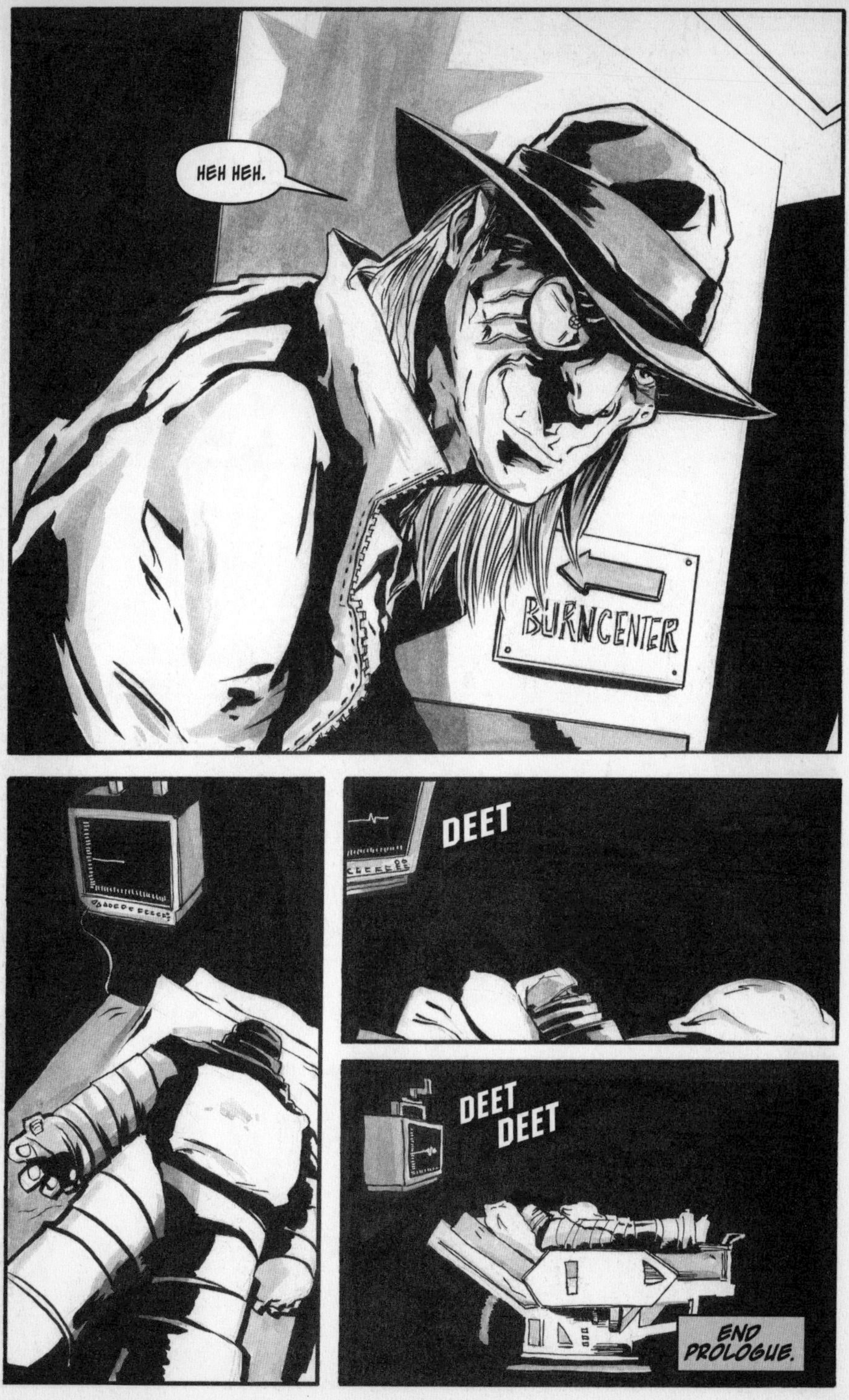
HEH HEH.
BURNCENTER
DEET
DEET
DEET
END PROLOGUE.

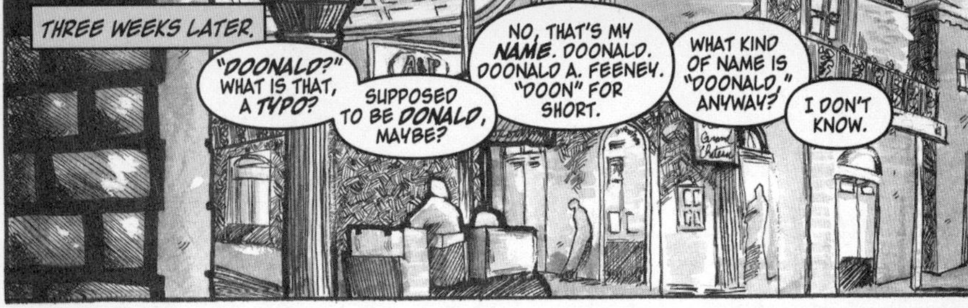
THREE WEEKS LATER.
"DOONALD?" WHAT IS THAT, A TYPO?
SUPPOSED TO BE DONALD, MAYBE?
NO, THAT'S MY NAME. DOONALD. DOONALD A. FEENEY. "DOON" FOR SHORT.
WHAT KIND OF NAME IS "DOONALD," ANYWAY?
I DON'T KNOW.

# Chapter One: DOON

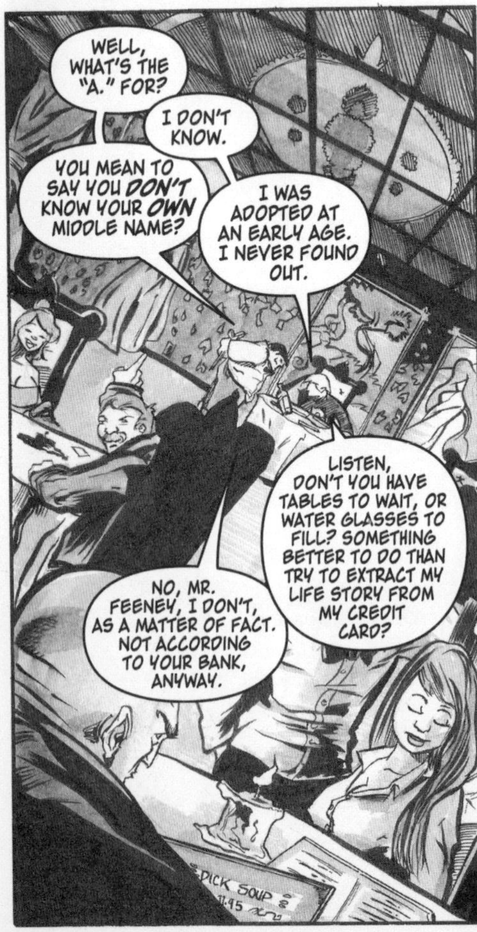
WELL, WHAT'S THE "A." FOR?
I DON'T KNOW.
YOU MEAN TO SAY YOU DON'T KNOW YOUR OWN MIDDLE NAME?
I WAS ADOPTED AT AN EARLY AGE. I NEVER FOUND OUT.
LISTEN, DON'T YOU HAVE TABLES TO WAIT, OR WATER GLASSES TO FILL? SOMETHING BETTER TO DO THAN TRY TO EXTRACT MY LIFE STORY FROM MY CREDIT CARD?
NO, MR. FEENEY, I DON'T, AS A MATTER OF FACT. NOT ACCORDING TO YOUR BANK, ANYWAY.

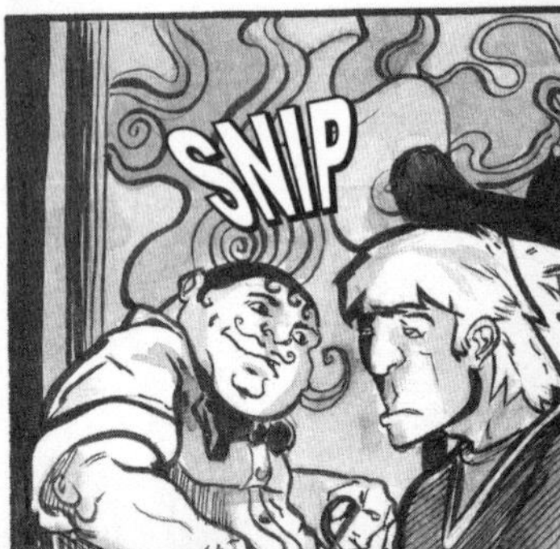
SNIP

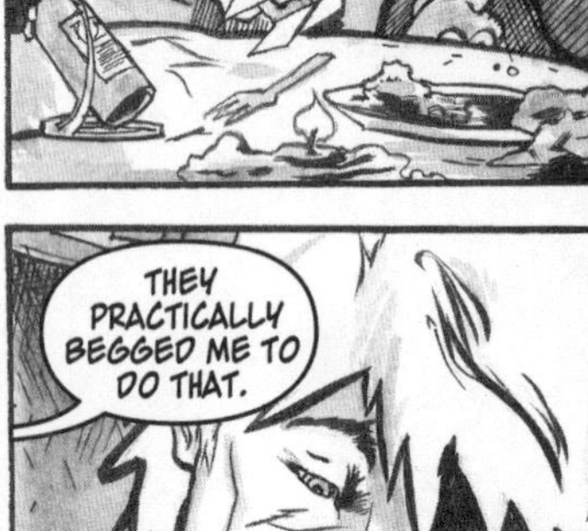
THEY PRACTICALLY BEGGED ME TO DO THAT.

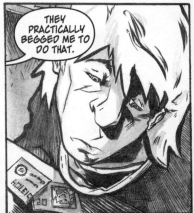

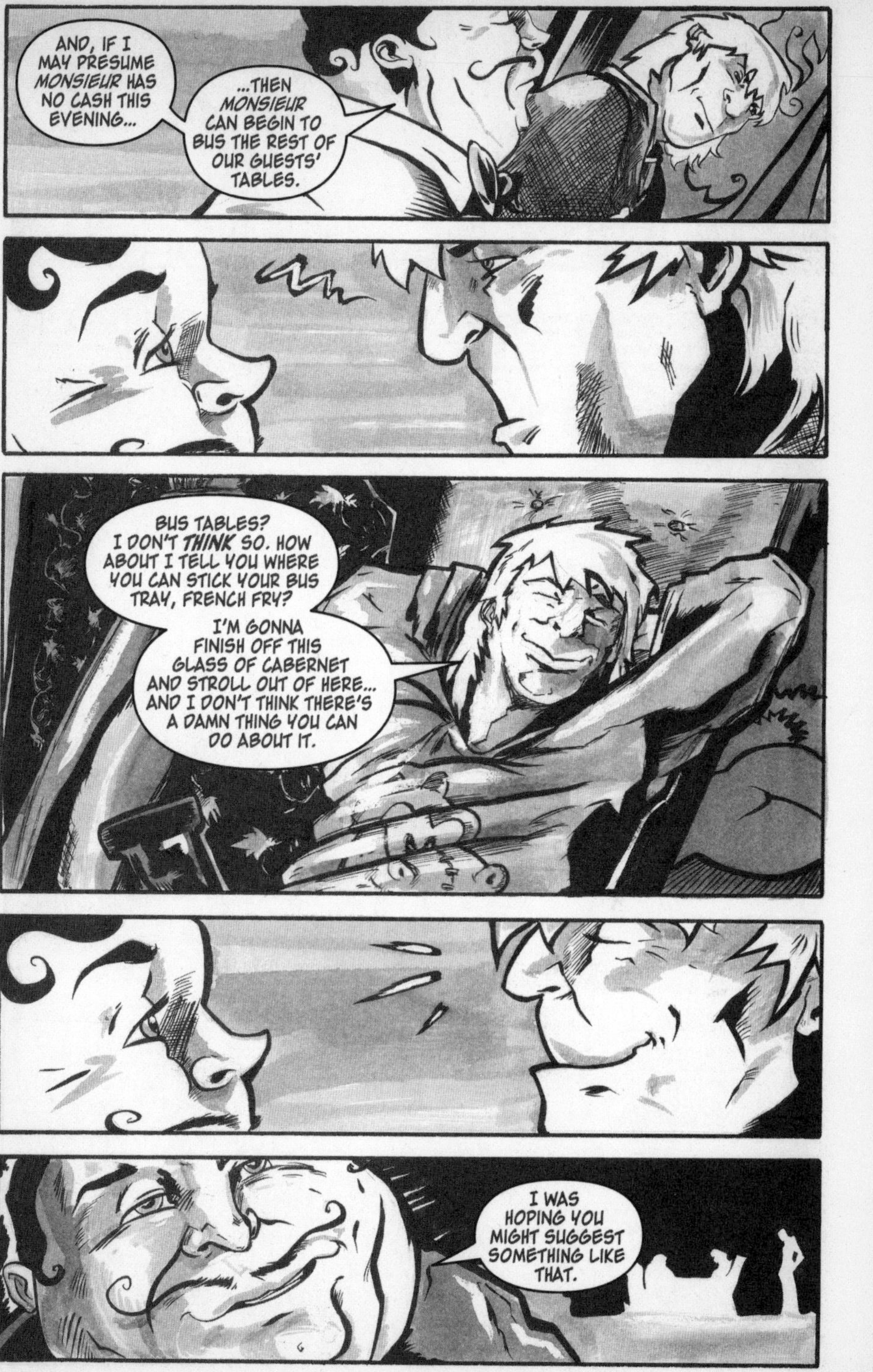
AND, IF I MAY PRESUME MONSIEUR HAS NO CASH THIS EVENING...
...THEN MONSIEUR CAN BEGIN TO BUS THE REST OF OUR GUESTS' TABLES.
BUS TABLES? I DON'T THINK SO. HOW ABOUT I TELL YOU WHERE YOU CAN STICK YOUR BUS TRAY, FRENCH FRY?
I'M GONNA FINISH OFF THIS GLASS OF CABERNET AND STROLL OUT OF HERE... AND I DON'T THINK THERE'S A DAMN THING YOU CAN DO ABOUT IT.
I WAS HOPING YOU MIGHT SUGGEST SOMETHING LIKE THAT.

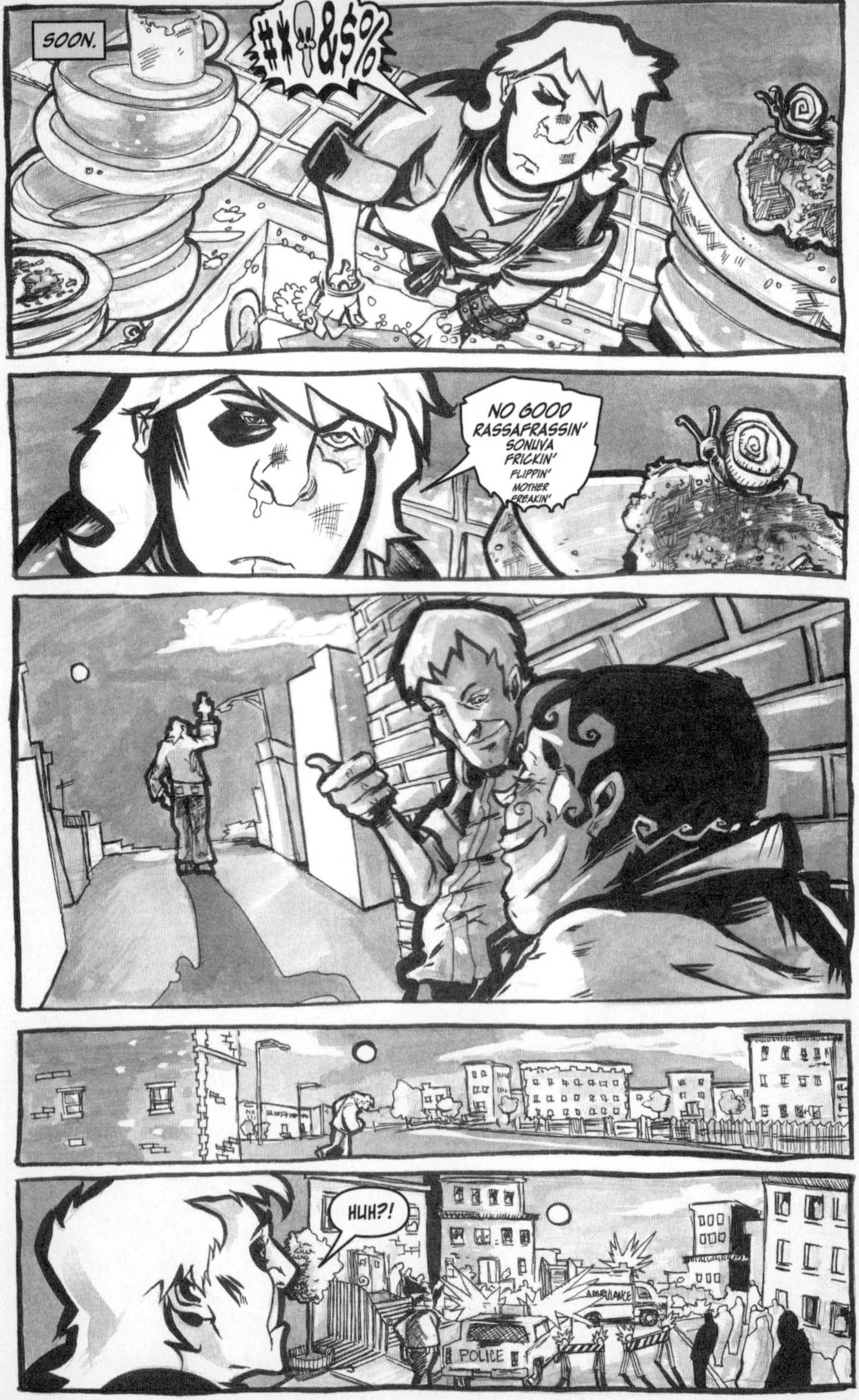
SOON.
#*&$%
NO GOOD RASSAFRASSIN' SONUVA FRICKIN' FLIPPIN' MOTHER FREAKIN'
HUH?!
AMBULANCE
POLICE

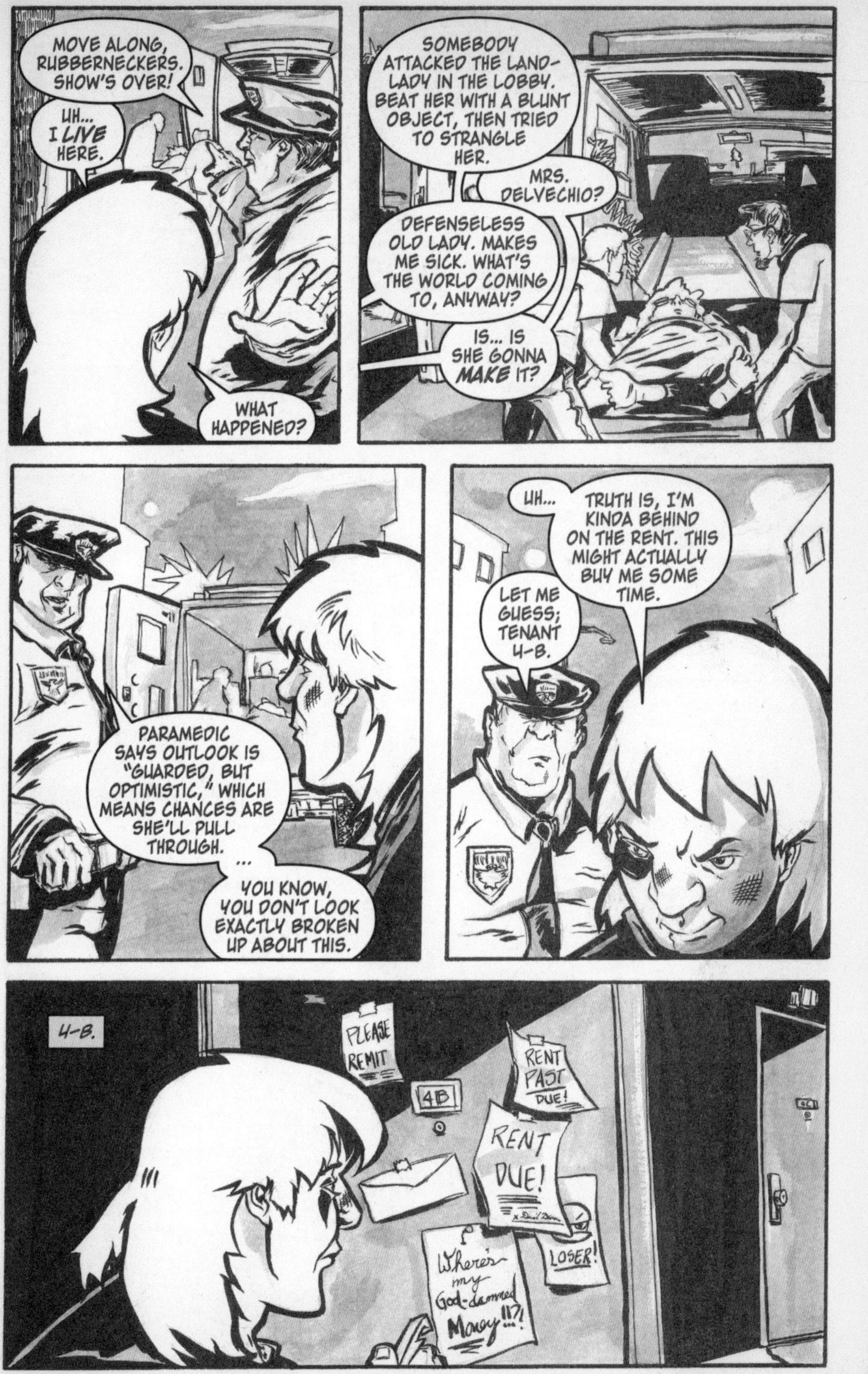
MOVE ALONG, RUBBERNECKERS. SHOW'S OVER!
UH... I LIVE HERE.
WHAT HAPPENED?
SOMEBODY ATTACKED THE LAND-LADY IN THE LOBBY. BEAT HER WITH A BLUNT OBJECT, THEN TRIED TO STRANGLE HER.
MRS. DELVECHIO?
DEFENSELESS OLD LADY. MAKES ME SICK. WHAT'S THE WORLD COMING TO, ANYWAY?
IS... IS SHE GONNA MAKE IT?
PARAMEDIC SAYS OUTLOOK IS "GUARDED, BUT OPTIMISTIC," WHICH MEANS CHANCES ARE SHE'LL PULL THROUGH.
...
YOU KNOW, YOU DON'T LOOK EXACTLY BROKEN UP ABOUT THIS.
UH...
TRUTH IS, I'M KINDA BEHIND ON THE RENT. THIS MIGHT ACTUALLY BUY ME SOME TIME.
LET ME GUESS; TENANT 4-B.
4-B.
PLEASE REMIT
4B
RENT PAST DUE!
RENT DUE!
LOSER!
Where's my God-damned Money!!?!...

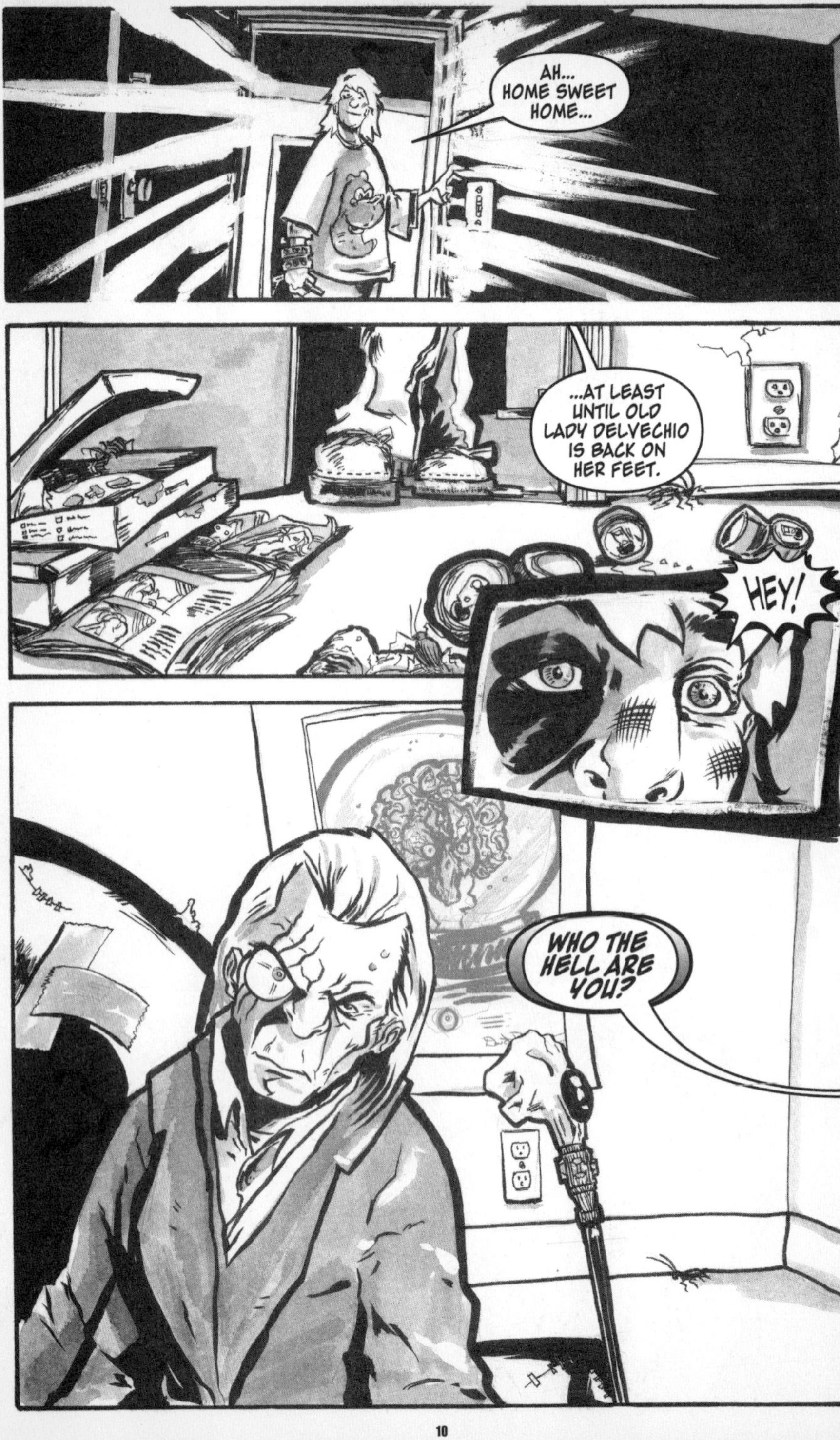
AH... HOME SWEET HOME...
...AT LEAST UNTIL OLD LADY DELVECHIO IS BACK ON HER FEET.
HEY!
WHO THE HELL ARE YOU?

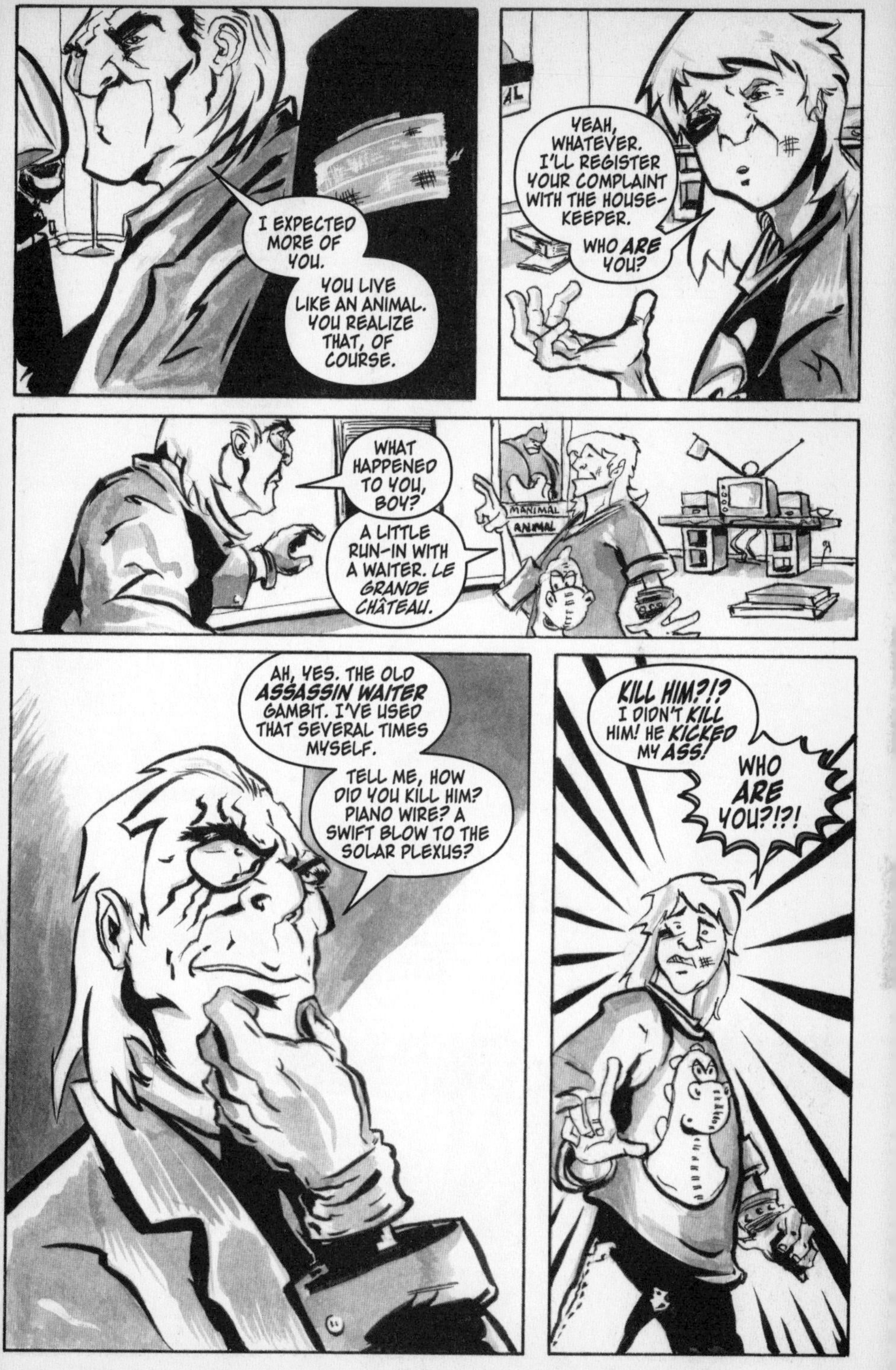
I EXPECTED MORE OF YOU.
YOU LIVE LIKE AN ANIMAL. YOU REALIZE THAT, OF COURSE.
YEAH, WHATEVER. I'LL REGISTER YOUR COMPLAINT WITH THE HOUSE-KEEPER.
WHO ARE YOU?
WHAT HAPPENED TO YOU, BOY?
A LITTLE RUN-IN WITH A WAITER. LE GRANDE CHÂTEAU.
ANIMAL
AH, YES. THE OLD ASSASSIN WAITER GAMBIT. I'VE USED THAT SEVERAL TIMES MYSELF.
TELL ME, HOW DID YOU KILL HIM? PIANO WIRE? A SWIFT BLOW TO THE SOLAR PLEXUS?
KILL HIM?!? I DIDN'T KILL HIM! HE KICKED MY ASS!
WHO ARE YOU?!?!

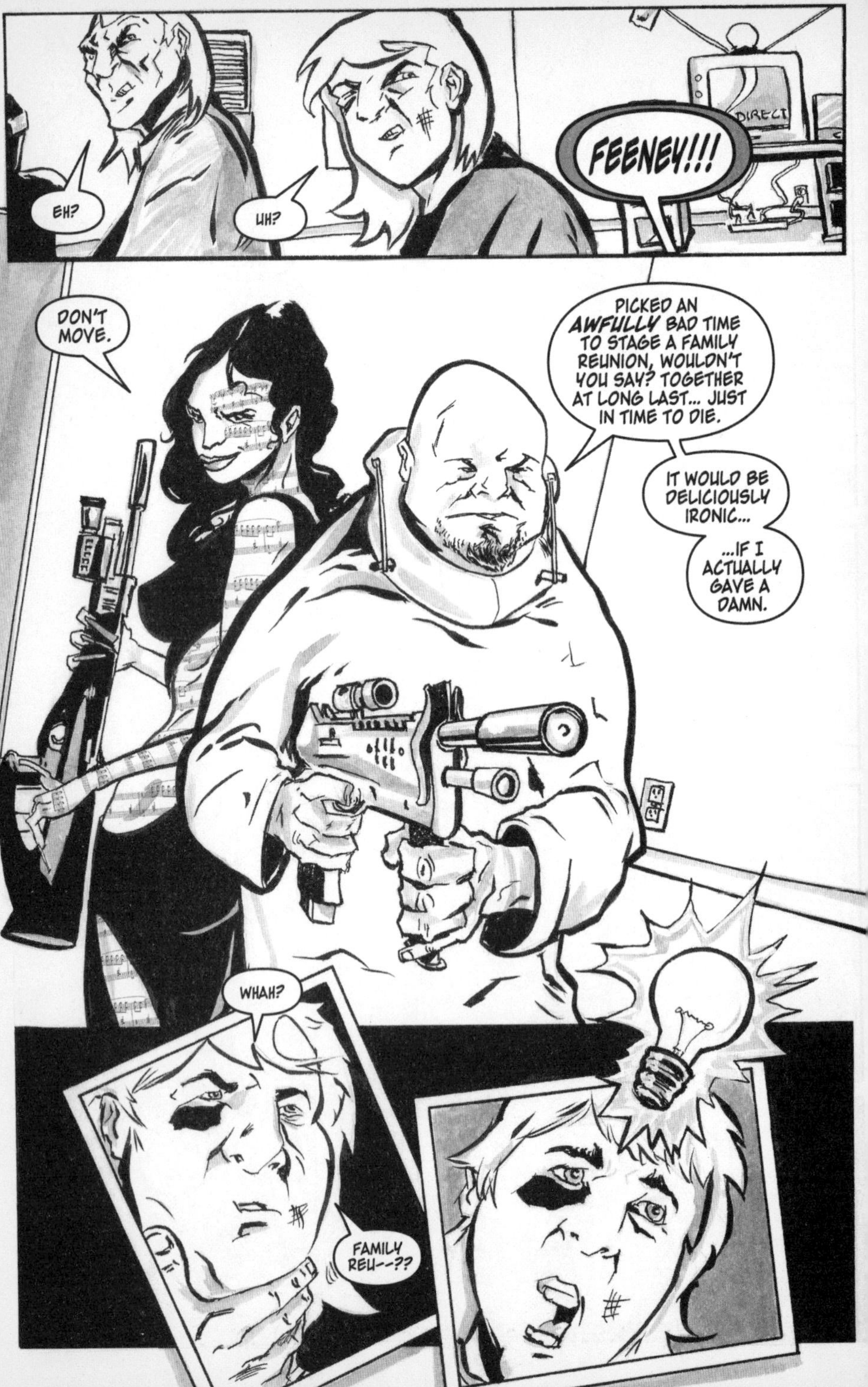
EH?
UH?
FEENEY!!!
DON'T MOVE.
PICKED AN AWFULLY BAD TIME TO STAGE A FAMILY REUNION, WOULDN'T YOU SAY? TOGETHER AT LONG LAST... JUST IN TIME TO DIE.
IT WOULD BE DELICIOUSLY IRONIC...
...IF I ACTUALLY GAVE A DAMN.
WHAH?
FAMILY REU--??
DIRECT

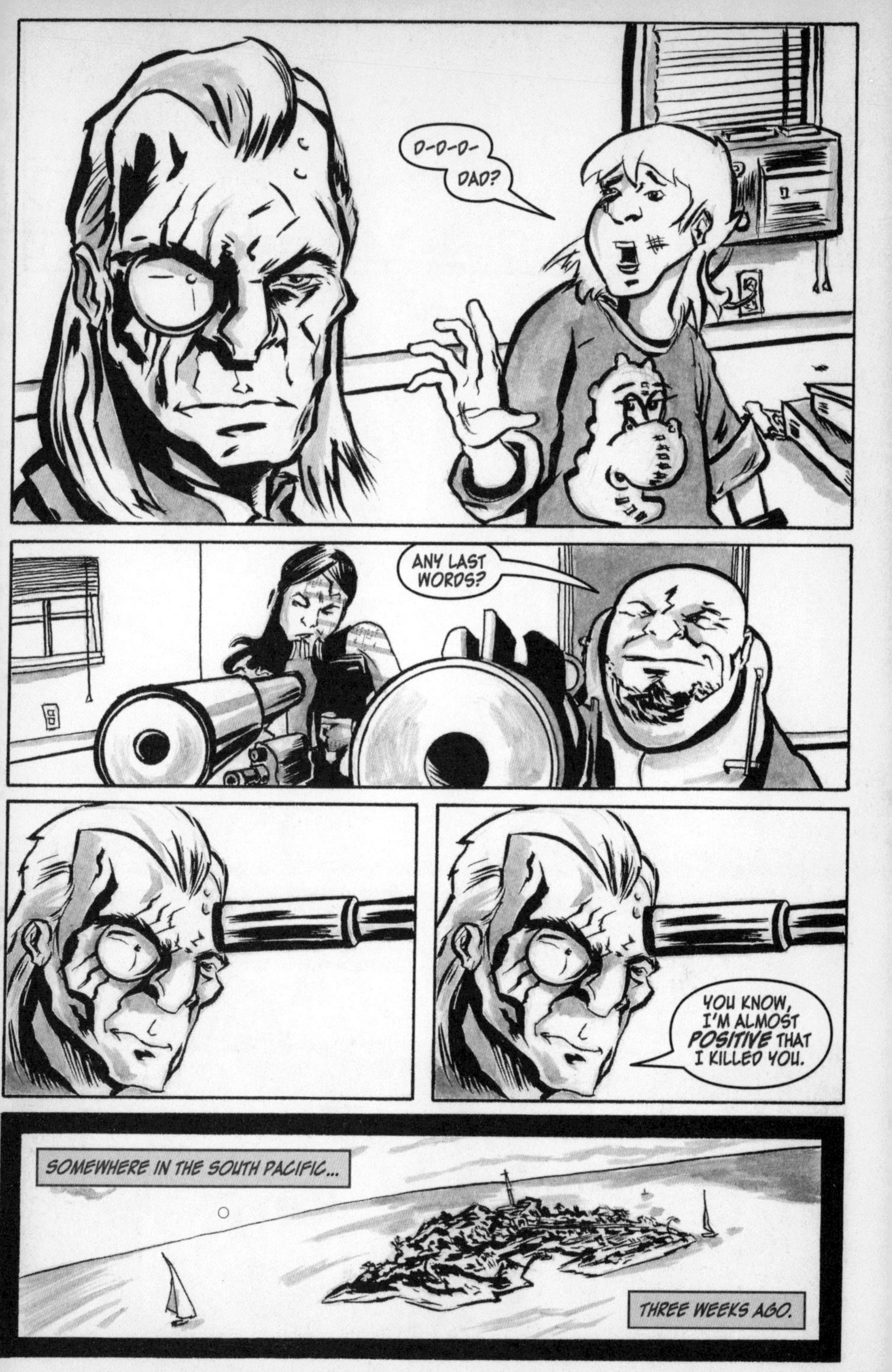
D-D-D-
DAD?
ANY LAST WORDS?
YOU KNOW, I'M ALMOST POSITIVE THAT I KILLED YOU.
SOMEWHERE IN THE SOUTH PACIFIC...
THREE WEEKS AGO.

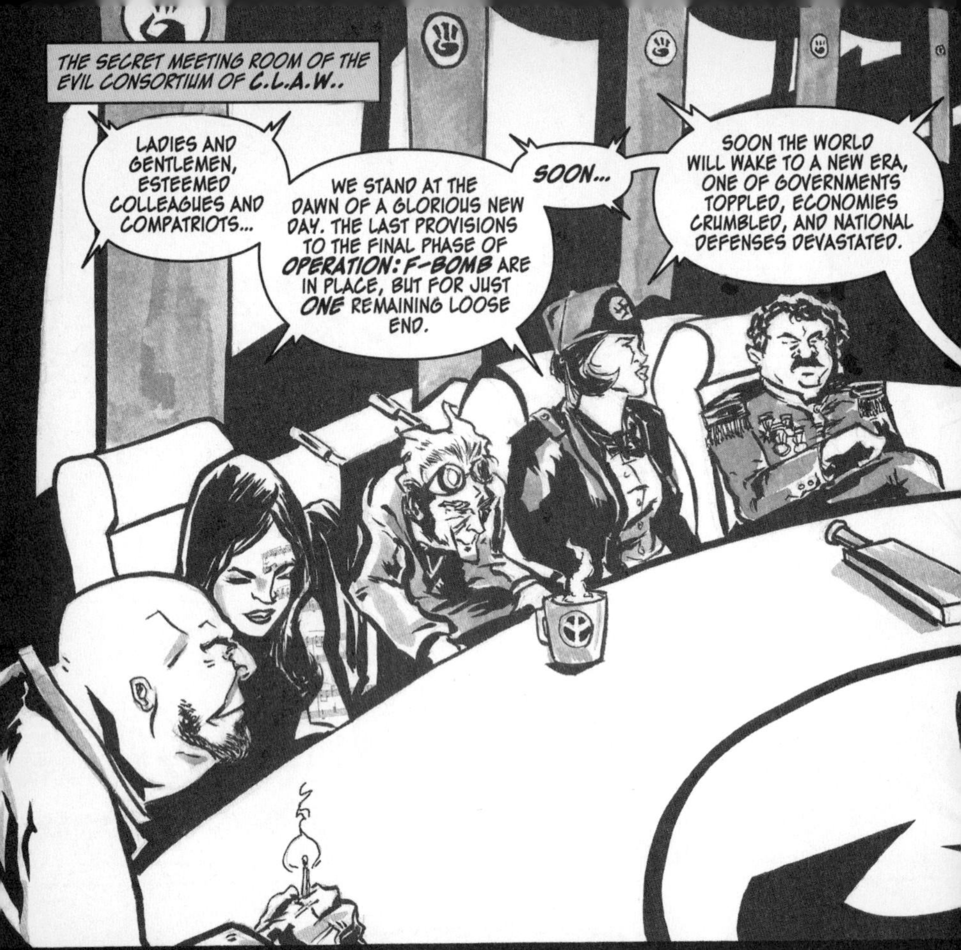
THE SECRET MEETING ROOM OF THE EVIL CONSORTIUM OF C.L.A.W..
LADIES AND GENTLEMEN, ESTEEMED COLLEAGUES AND COMPATRIOTS...
WE STAND AT THE DAWN OF A GLORIOUS NEW DAY. THE LAST PROVISIONS TO THE FINAL PHASE OF OPERATION: F-BOMB ARE IN PLACE, BUT FOR JUST ONE REMAINING LOOSE END.
SOON...
SOON THE WORLD WILL WAKE TO A NEW ERA, ONE OF GOVERNMENTS TOPPLED, ECONOMIES CRUMBLED, AND NATIONAL DEFENSES DEVASTATED.

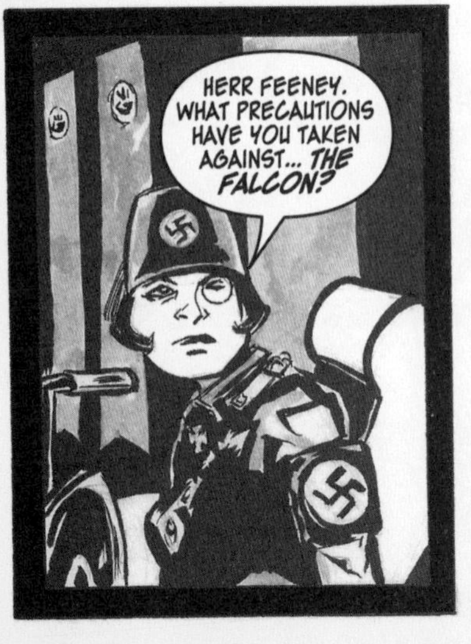
HERR FEENEY. WHAT PRECAUTIONS HAVE YOU TAKEN AGAINST... THE FALCON?

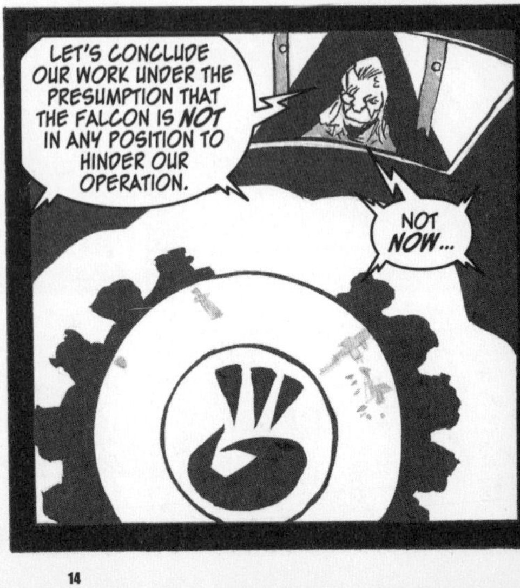
LET'S CONCLUDE OUR WORK UNDER THE PRESUMPTION THAT THE FALCON IS NOT IN ANY POSITION TO HINDER OUR OPERATION.
NOT NOW...

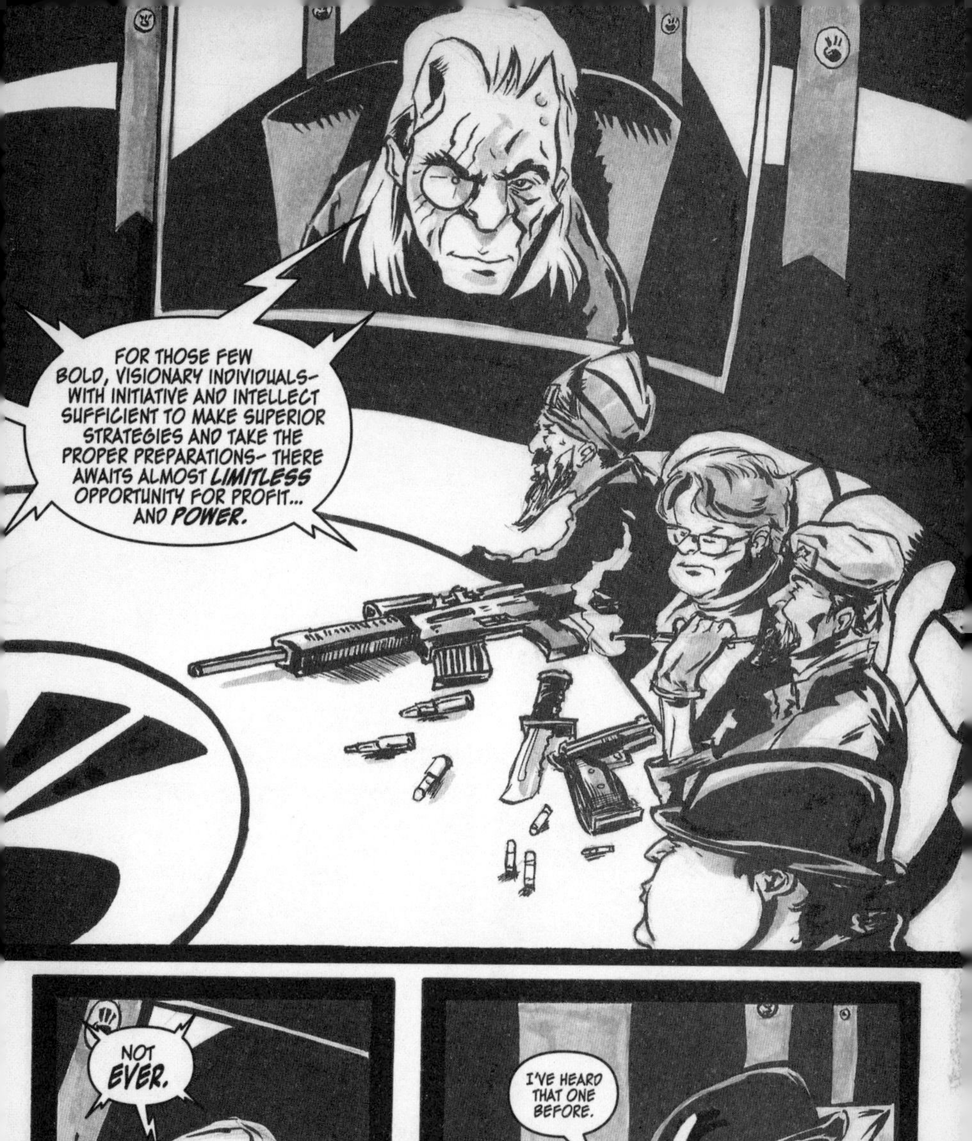
FOR THOSE FEW BOLD, VISIONARY INDIVIDUALS- WITH INITIATIVE AND INTELLECT SUFFICIENT TO MAKE SUPERIOR STRATEGIES AND TAKE THE PROPER PREPARATIONS- THERE AWAITS ALMOST *LIMITLESS* OPPORTUNITY FOR PROFIT... AND *POWER.*

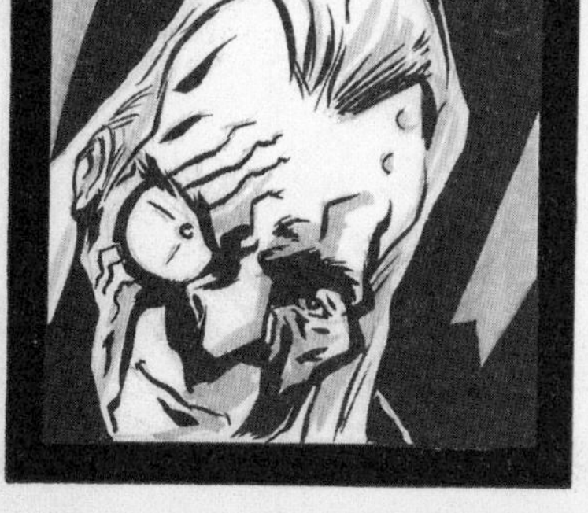
NOT *EVER.*

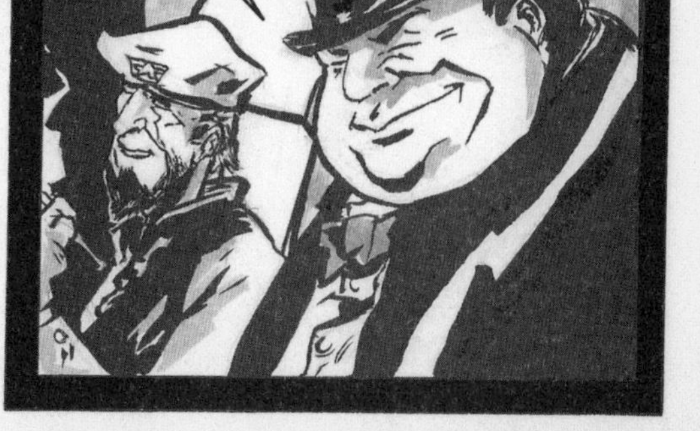
I'VE HEARD THAT ONE BEFORE.

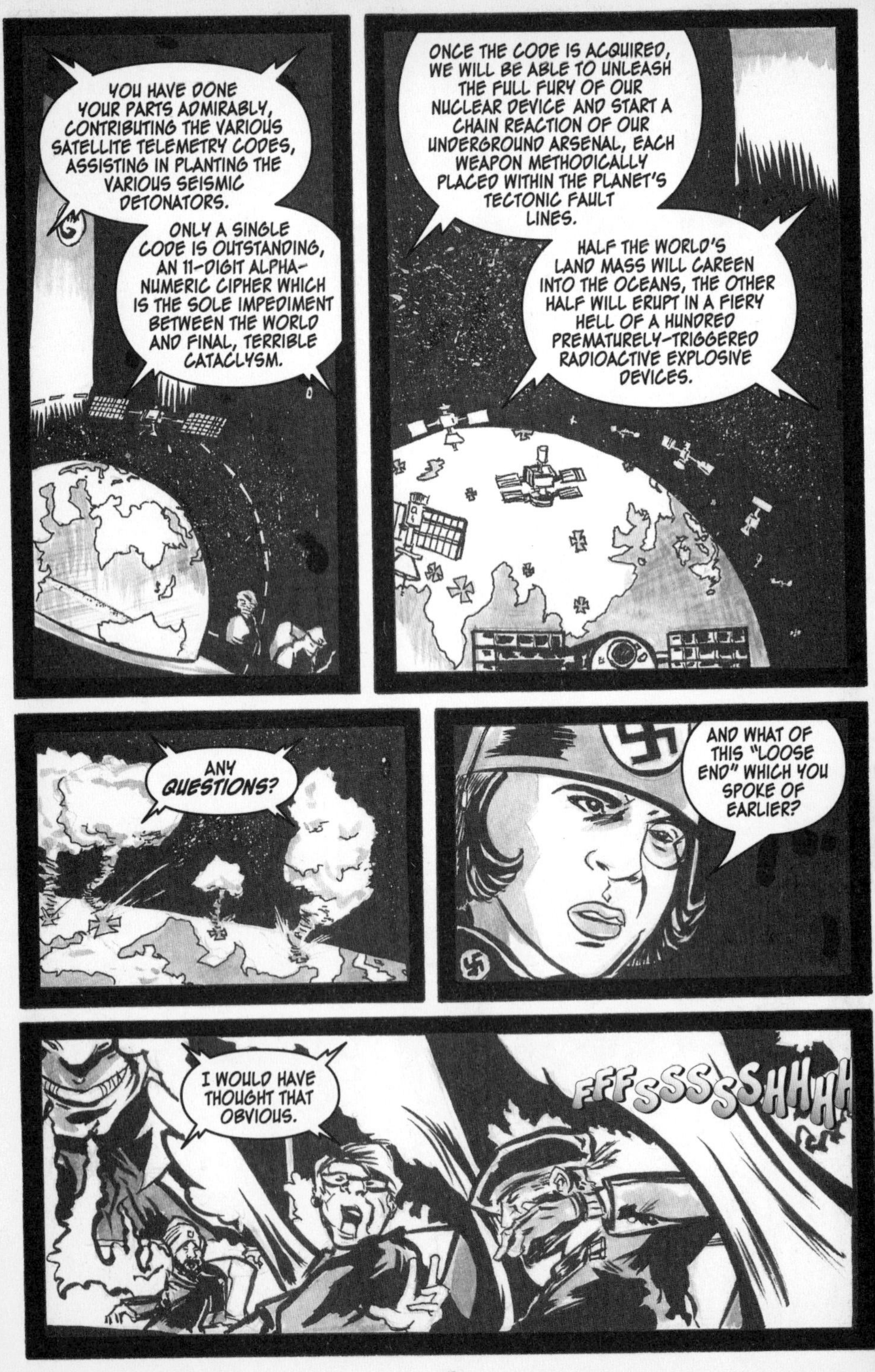
YOU HAVE DONE YOUR PARTS ADMIRABLY, CONTRIBUTING THE VARIOUS SATELLITE TELEMETRY CODES, ASSISTING IN PLANTING THE VARIOUS SEISMIC DETONATORS.
ONLY A SINGLE CODE IS OUTSTANDING, AN 11-DIGIT ALPHA-NUMERIC CIPHER WHICH IS THE SOLE IMPEDIMENT BETWEEN THE WORLD AND FINAL, TERRIBLE CATACLYSM.
ONCE THE CODE IS ACQUIRED, WE WILL BE ABLE TO UNLEASH THE FULL FURY OF OUR NUCLEAR DEVICE AND START A CHAIN REACTION OF OUR UNDERGROUND ARSENAL, EACH WEAPON METHODICALLY PLACED WITHIN THE PLANET'S TECTONIC FAULT LINES.
HALF THE WORLD'S LAND MASS WILL CAREEN INTO THE OCEANS, THE OTHER HALF WILL ERUPT IN A FIERY HELL OF A HUNDRED PREMATURELY-TRIGGERED RADIOACTIVE EXPLOSIVE DEVICES.
ANY QUESTIONS?
AND WHAT OF THIS "LOOSE END" WHICH YOU SPOKE OF EARLIER?
I WOULD HAVE THOUGHT THAT OBVIOUS.
FFFSSSSSHHHH

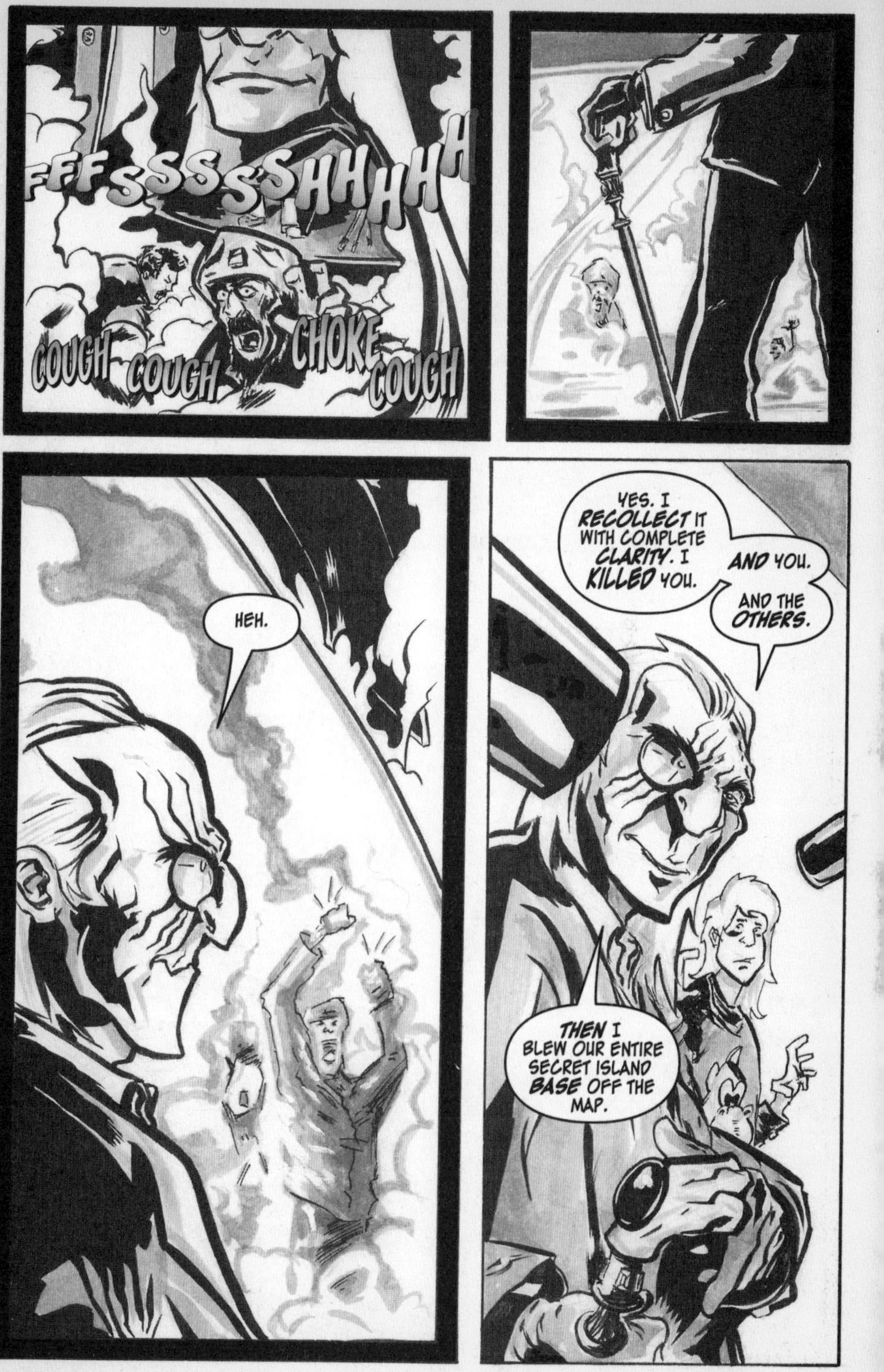
FFFSSSSSHHHHH
COUGH COUGH
CHOKE COUGH
HEH.
YES. I RECOLLECT IT WITH COMPLETE CLARITY. I KILLED YOU.
AND YOU.
AND THE OTHERS.
THEN I BLEW OUR ENTIRE SECRET ISLAND BASE OFF THE MAP.

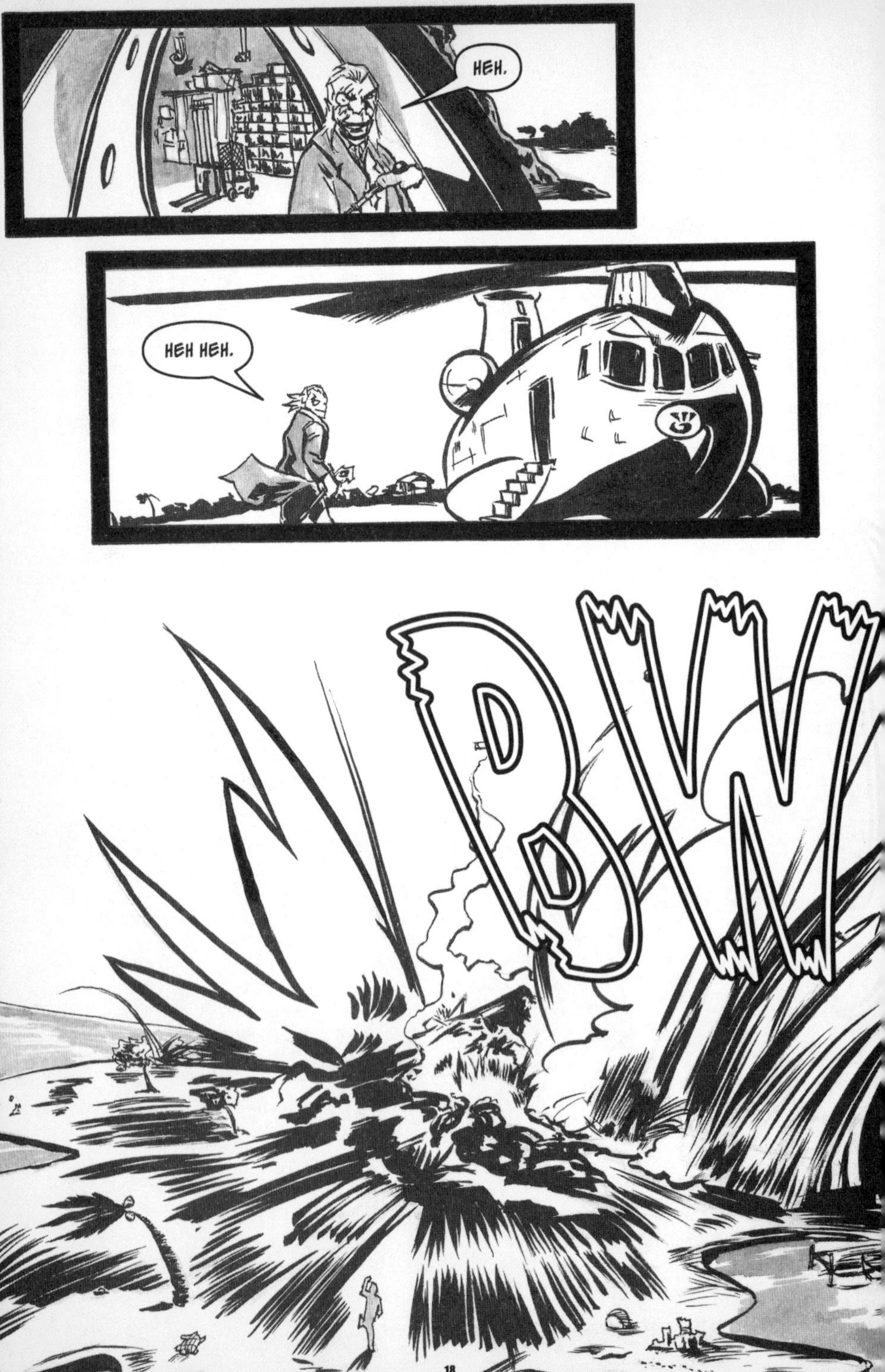
HEH.
HEH HEH.
BW

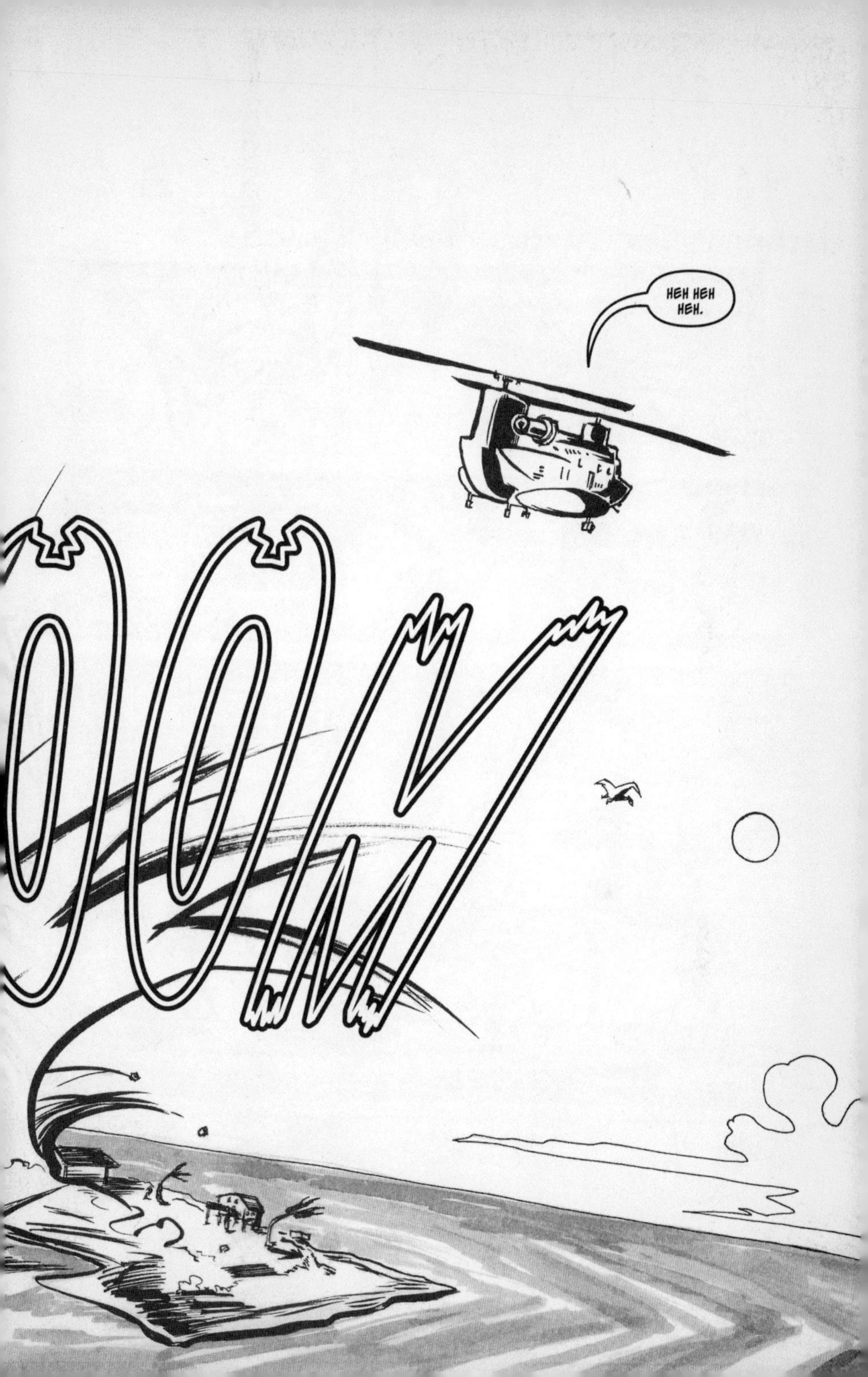
HEH HEH HEH.
OOM

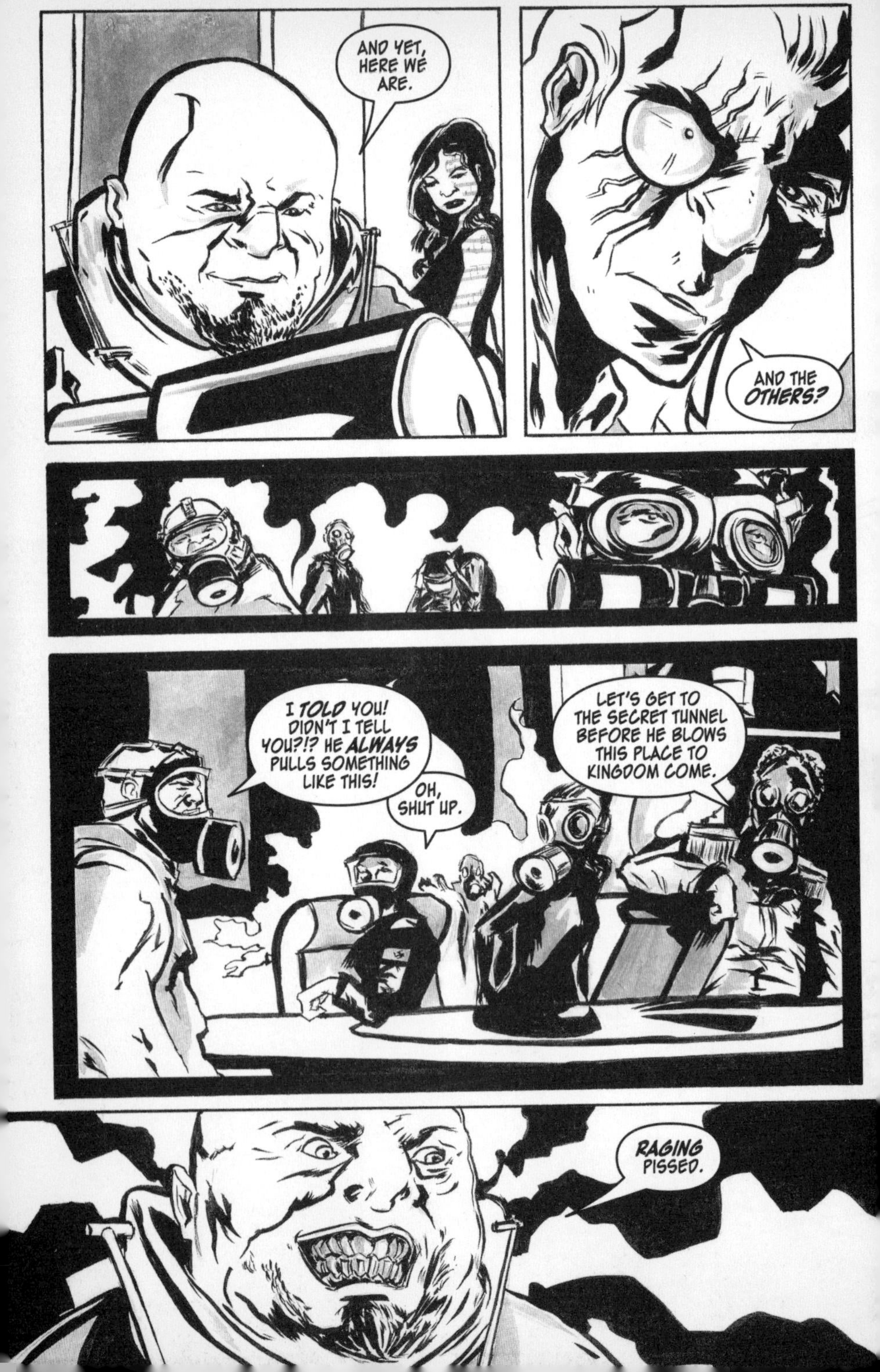
AND YET, HERE WE ARE.
AND THE OTHERS?
I TOLD YOU! DIDN'T I TELL YOU?!? HE ALWAYS PULLS SOMETHING LIKE THIS!
OH, SHUT UP.
LET'S GET TO THE SECRET TUNNEL BEFORE HE BLOWS THIS PLACE TO KINGDOM COME.
RAGING PISSED.

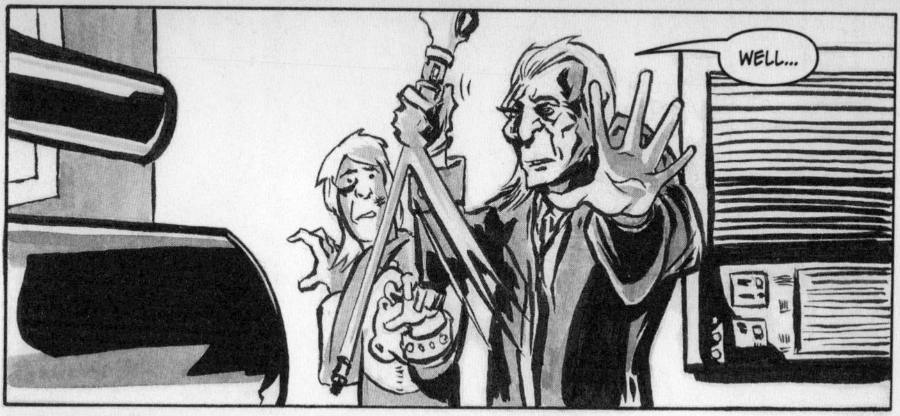
WELL...

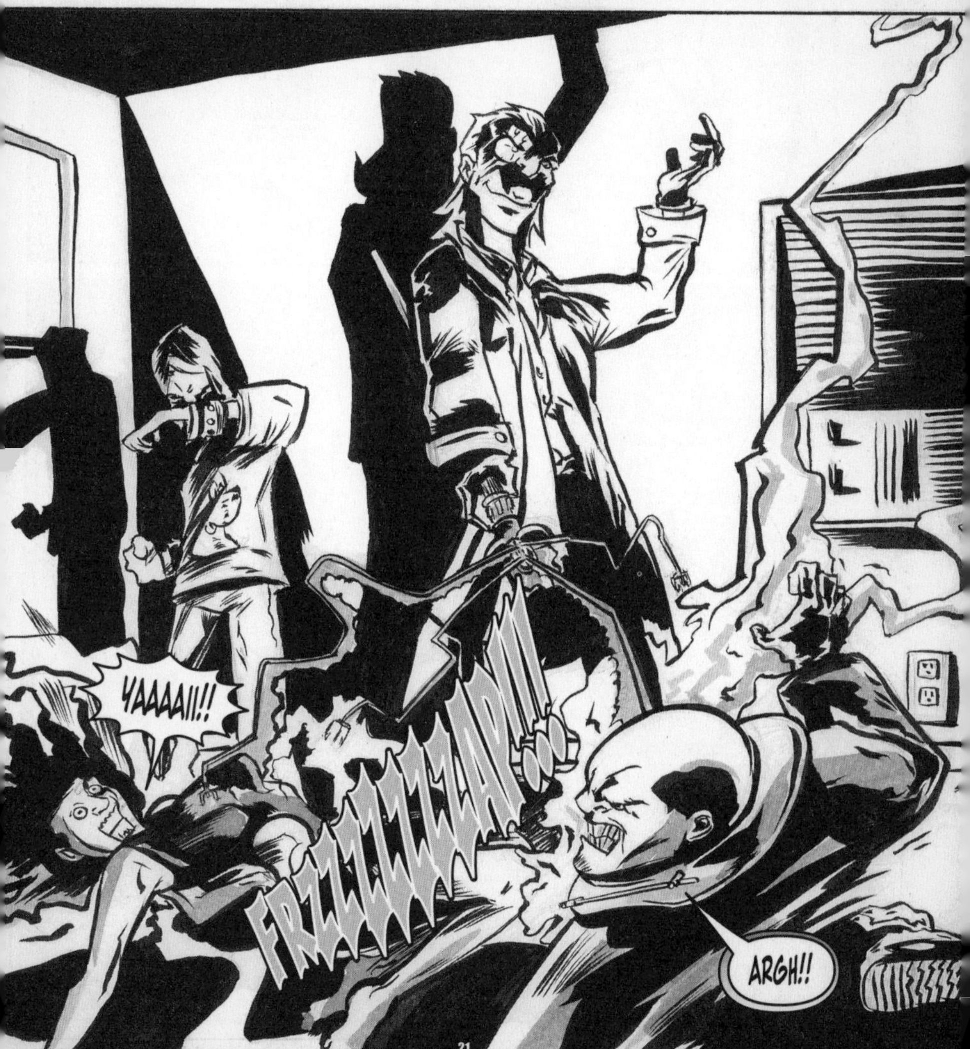
YAAAAII!!
FRZZZZZZZAP!!!...
ARGH!!

...THIS **COMPLICATES** THINGS.

A-A-ARE THEY... DEAD?

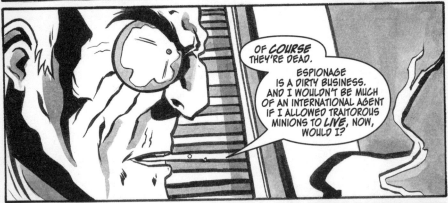

OF **COURSE** THEY'RE DEAD.

ESPIONAGE IS A **DIRTY** BUSINESS. AND I WOULDN'T BE MUCH OF AN INTERNATIONAL AGENT IF I ALLOWED TRAITOROUS MINIONS TO **LIVE**, NOW, WOULD I?

WHAT, YOU'RE, LIKE, SOME KIND OF **SPY**?

**DO** TRY TO KEEP UP, BOY. THIS ISN'T EXACTLY ROCKET SCIENCE.

THOUGH ROCKETS **WILL** BE INVOLVED. BIG, **GLORIOUS, NUCLEAR** ROCKETS, FIRED INTO THE WORLD'S TECTONIC PLATES, CREATING A RADIOACTIVE INFERNO OF DEATH AND DESTRUCTION.

AN **EVIL** SPY!?!

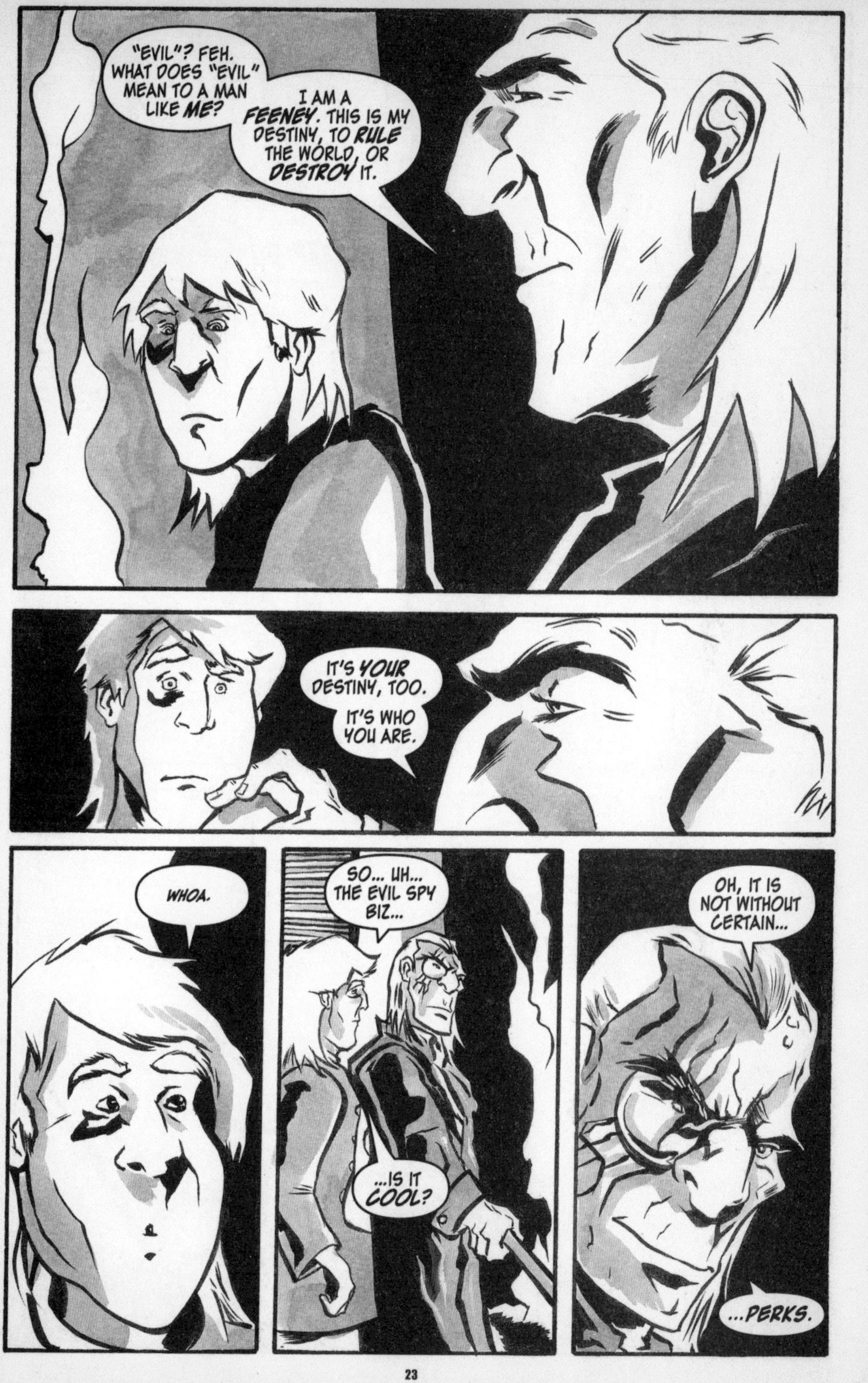
"EVIL"? FEH. WHAT DOES "EVIL" MEAN TO A MAN LIKE ME?
I AM A FEENEY. THIS IS MY DESTINY, TO RULE THE WORLD, OR DESTROY IT.
IT'S YOUR DESTINY, TOO.
IT'S WHO YOU ARE.
WHOA.
SO... UH... THE EVIL SPY BIZ...
...IS IT COOL?
OH, IT IS NOT WITHOUT CERTAIN...
...PERKS.

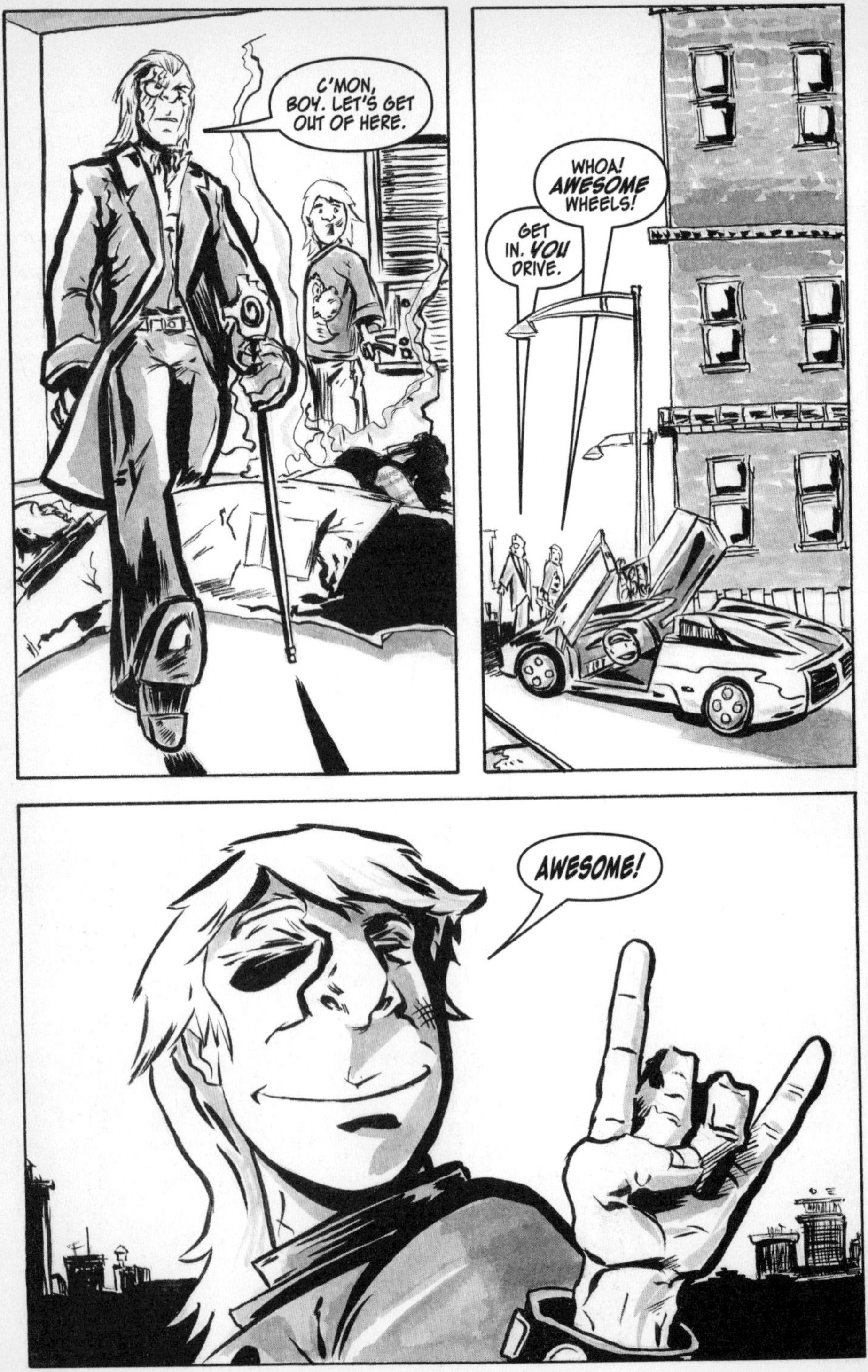
C'MON, BOY. LET'S GET OUT OF HERE.
WHOA! AWESOME WHEELS!
GET IN. YOU DRIVE.
AWESOME!

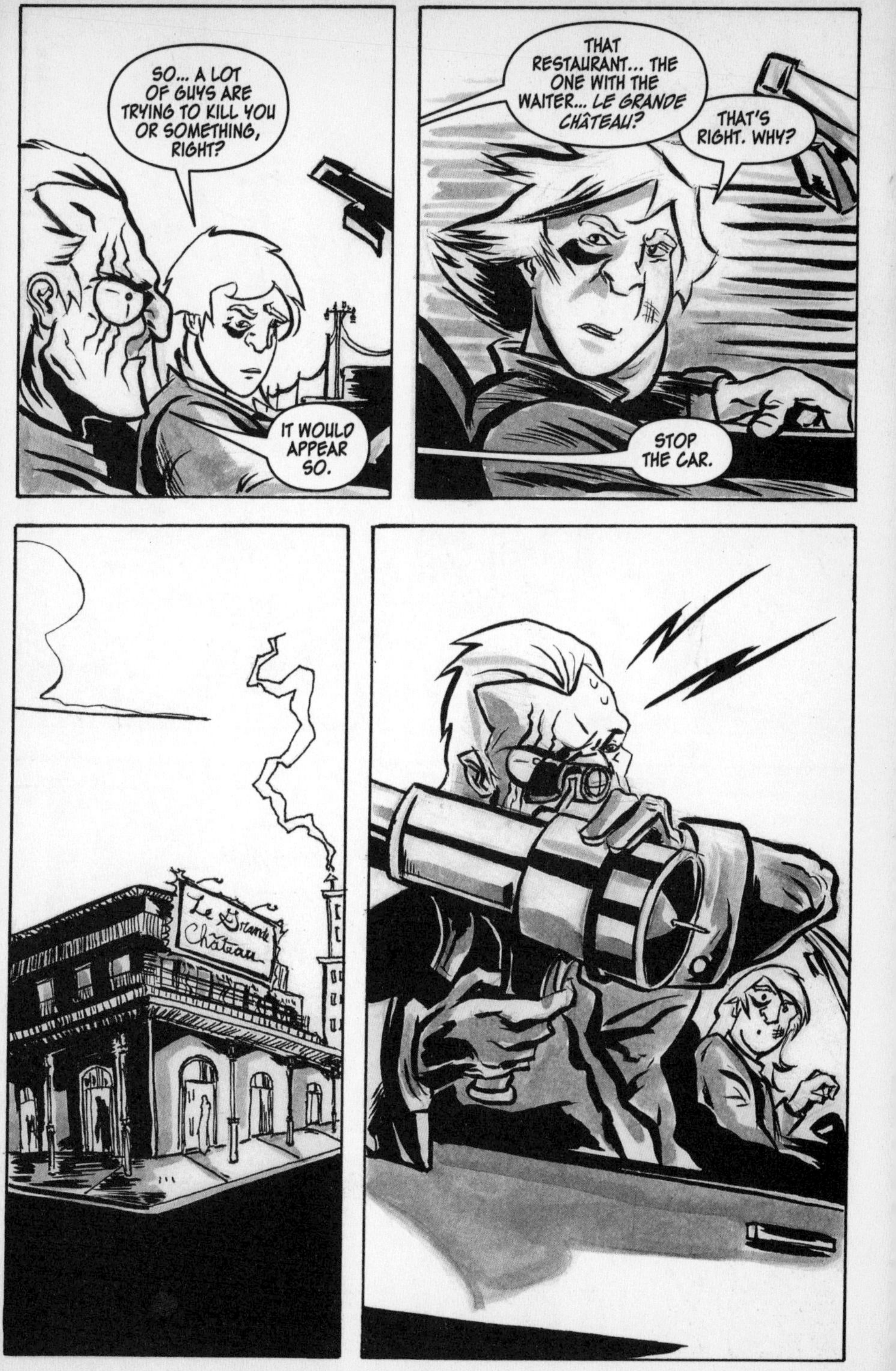
SO... A LOT OF GUYS ARE TRYING TO KILL YOU OR SOMETHING, RIGHT?
IT WOULD APPEAR SO.
THAT RESTAURANT... THE ONE WITH THE WAITER... LE GRANDE CHÂTEAU?
THAT'S RIGHT. WHY?
STOP THE CAR.
Le Grande Château

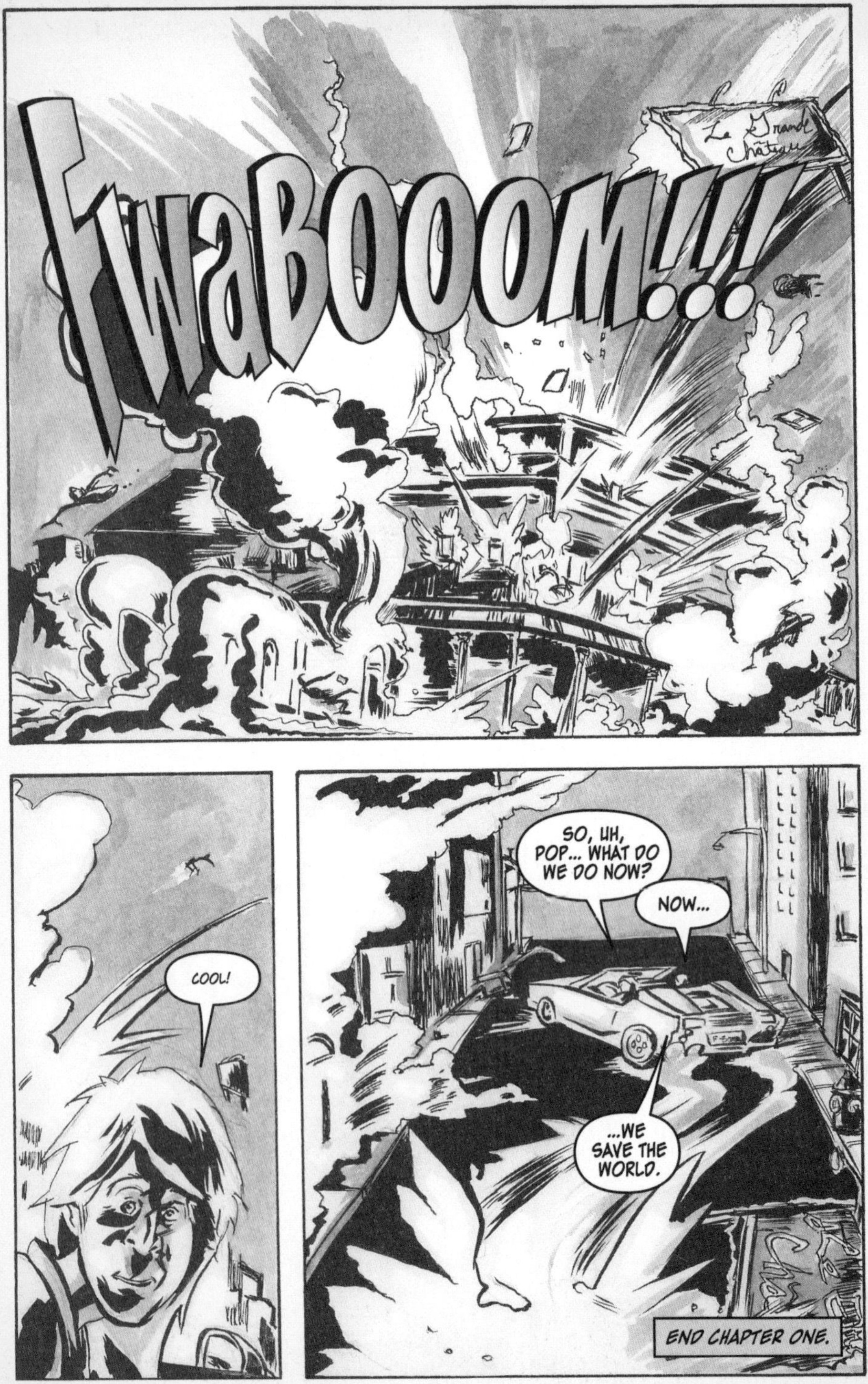
FWABOOOM!!!
Le Grande Château
COOL!
SO, UH, POP... WHAT DO WE DO NOW?
NOW...
...WE SAVE THE WORLD.
END CHAPTER ONE.

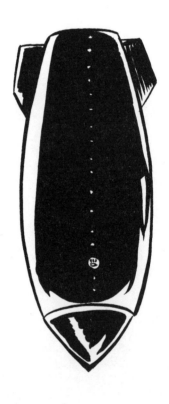

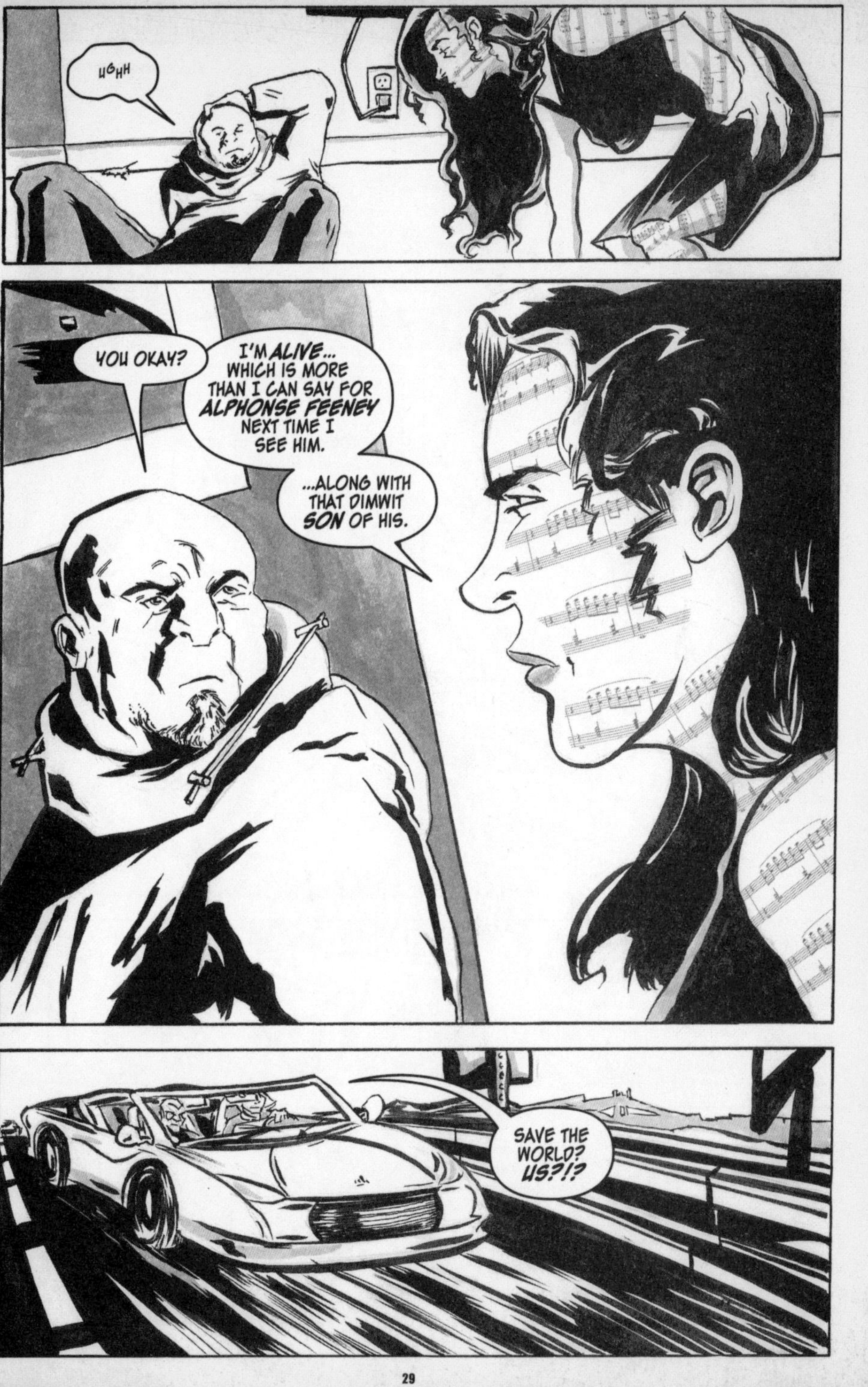
UGHH
YOU OKAY?
I'M ALIVE... WHICH IS MORE THAN I CAN SAY FOR ALPHONSE FEENEY NEXT TIME I SEE HIM.
...ALONG WITH THAT DIMWIT SON OF HIS.
SAVE THE WORLD? US?!?

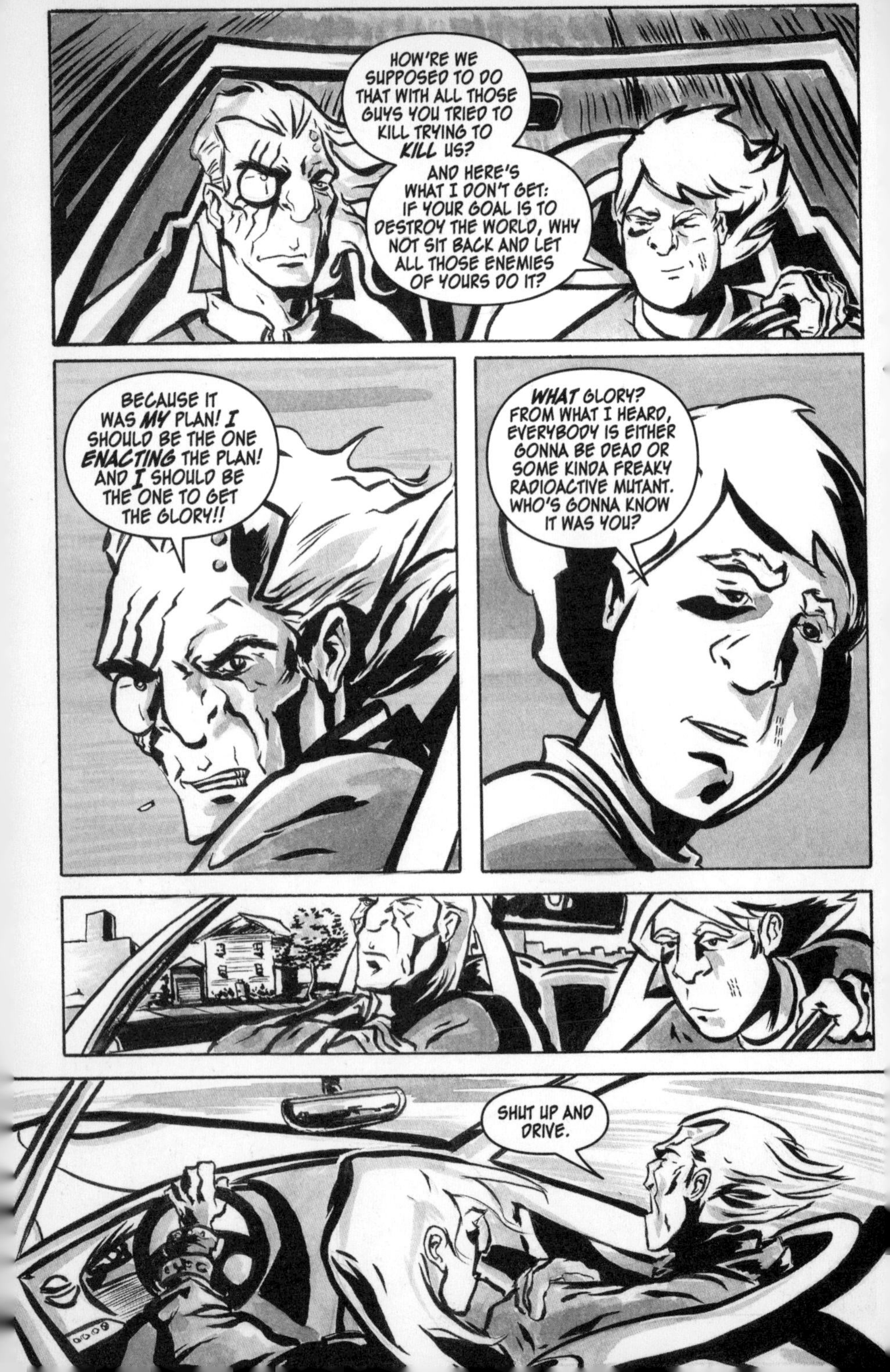
HOW'RE WE SUPPOSED TO DO THAT WITH ALL THOSE GUYS YOU TRIED TO KILL TRYING TO KILL US?
AND HERE'S WHAT I DON'T GET: IF YOUR GOAL IS TO DESTROY THE WORLD, WHY NOT SIT BACK AND LET ALL THOSE ENEMIES OF YOURS DO IT?
BECAUSE IT WAS MY PLAN! I SHOULD BE THE ONE ENACTING THE PLAN! AND I SHOULD BE THE ONE TO GET THE GLORY!!
WHAT GLORY? FROM WHAT I HEARD, EVERYBODY IS EITHER GONNA BE DEAD OR SOME KINDA FREAKY RADIOACTIVE MUTANT. WHO'S GONNA KNOW IT WAS YOU?
SHUT UP AND DRIVE.

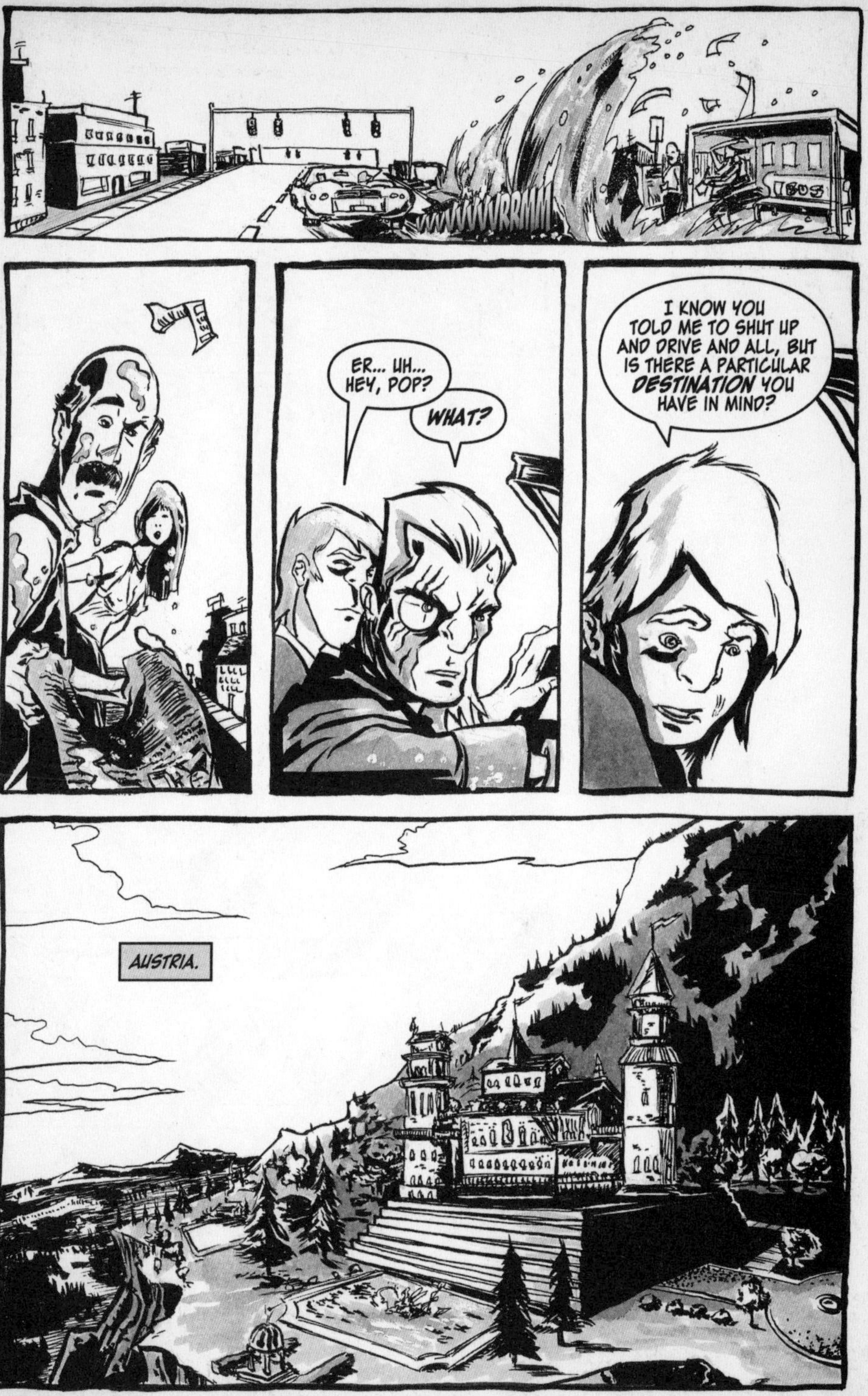
VVVVVVVVRRMM
ER... UH... HEY, POP?
WHAT?
I KNOW YOU TOLD ME TO SHUT UP AND DRIVE AND ALL, BUT IS THERE A PARTICULAR *DESTINATION* YOU HAVE IN MIND?
AUSTRIA.

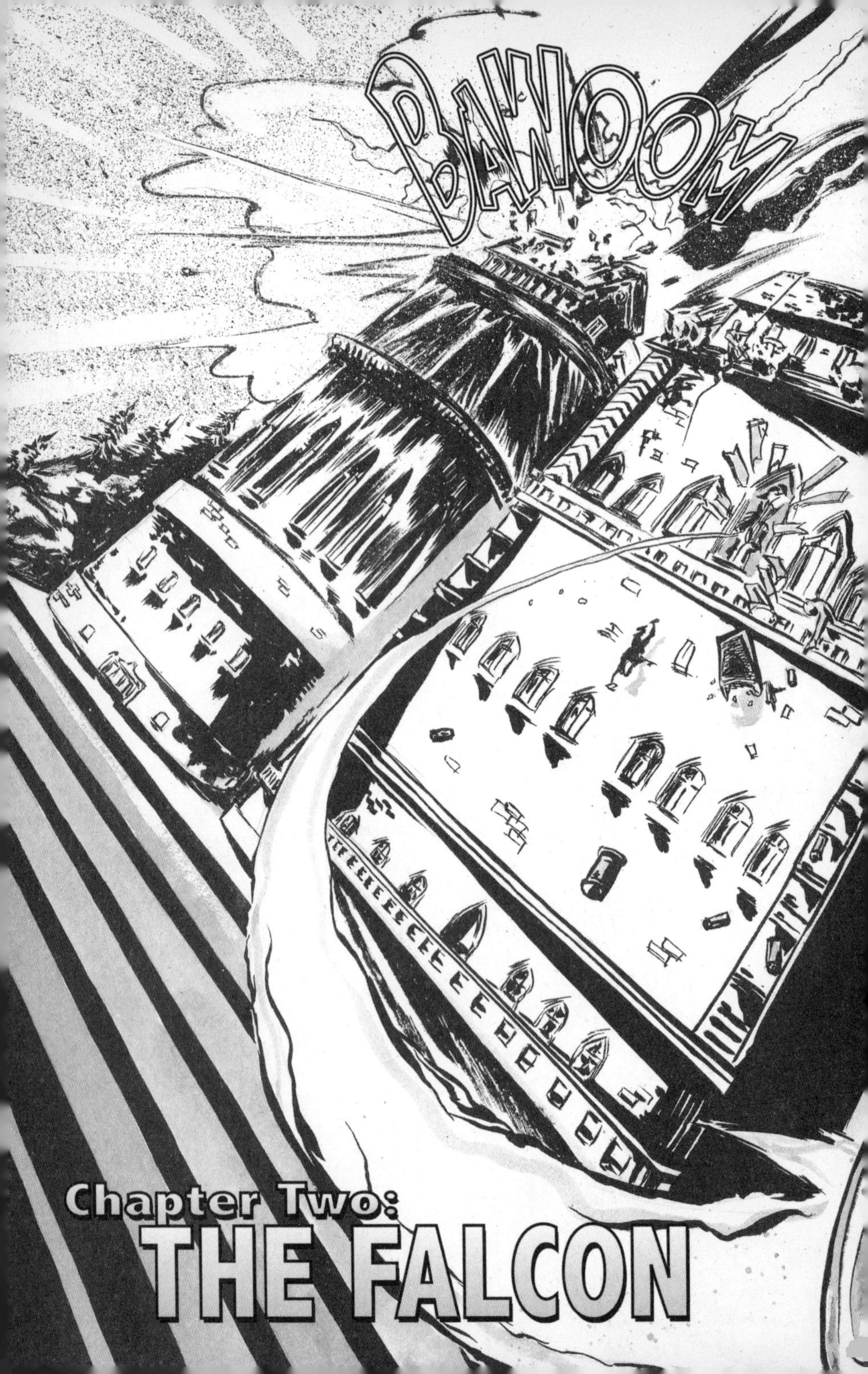
BAWOOM

# Chapter Two: THE FALCON

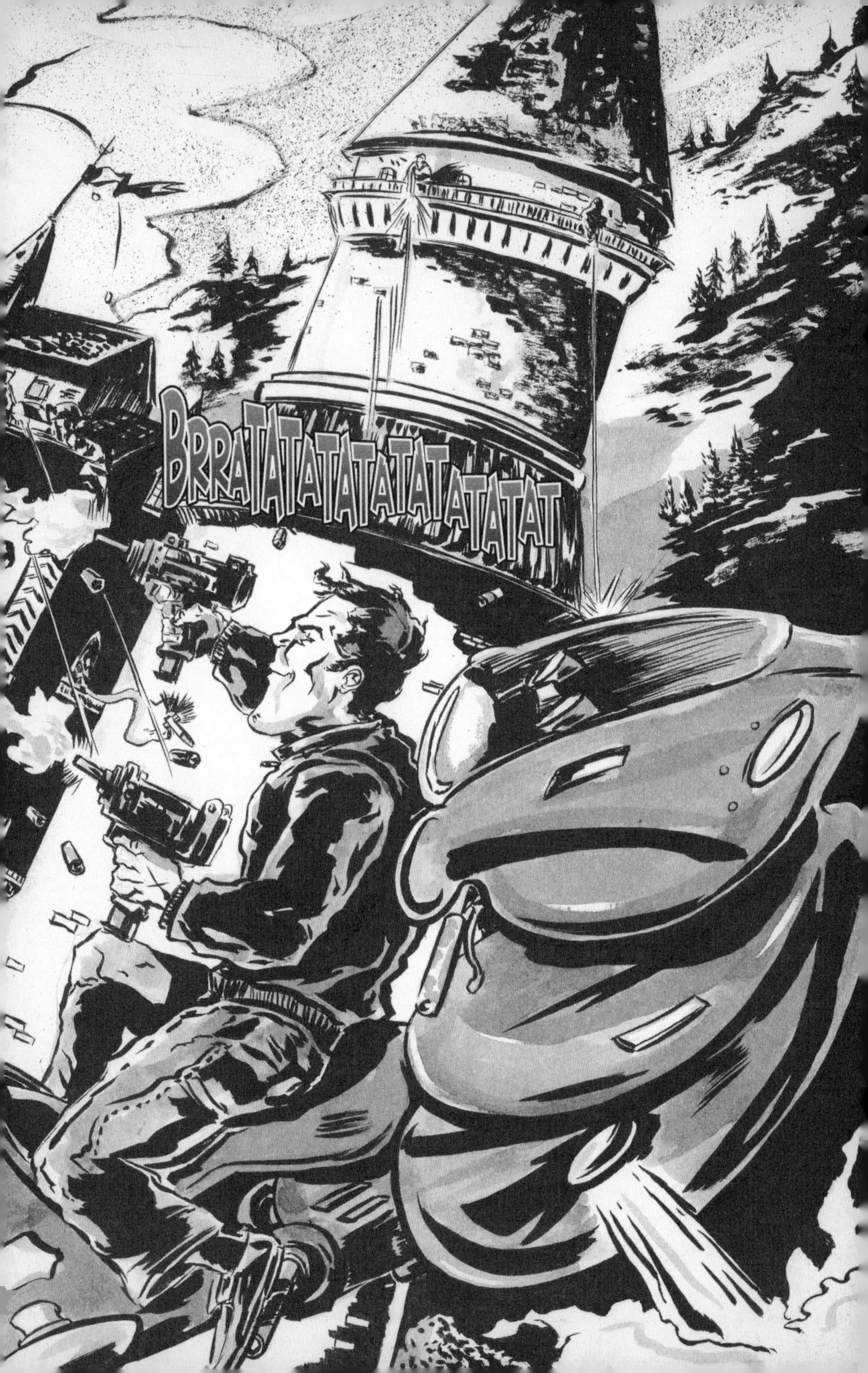
BRRATATATATATATATATAT

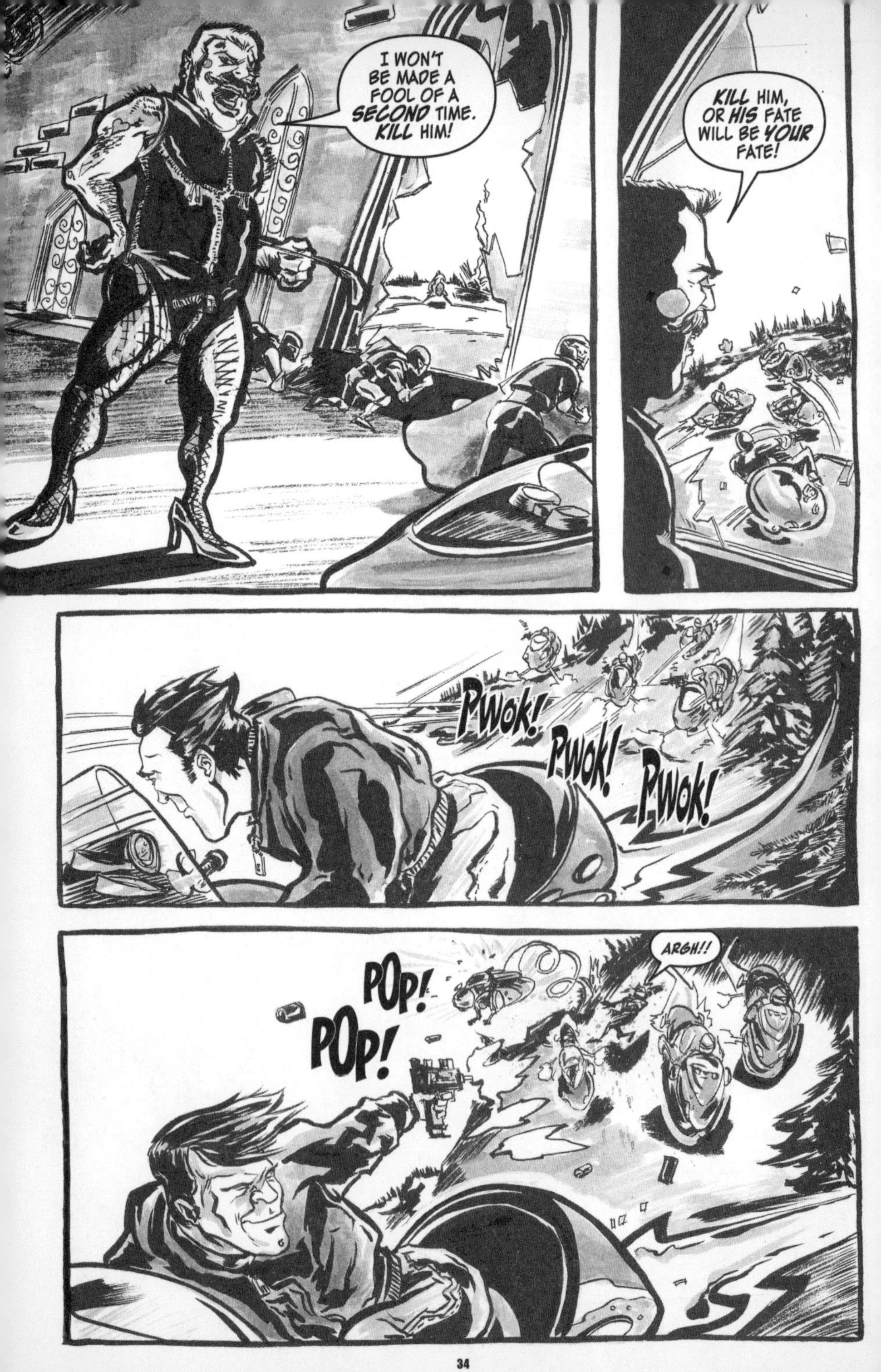

I WON'T BE MADE A FOOL OF A SECOND TIME. KILL HIM!
KILL HIM, OR HIS FATE WILL BE YOUR FATE!
PWOK!
PWOK!
PWOK!
POP!
POP!
ARGH!!

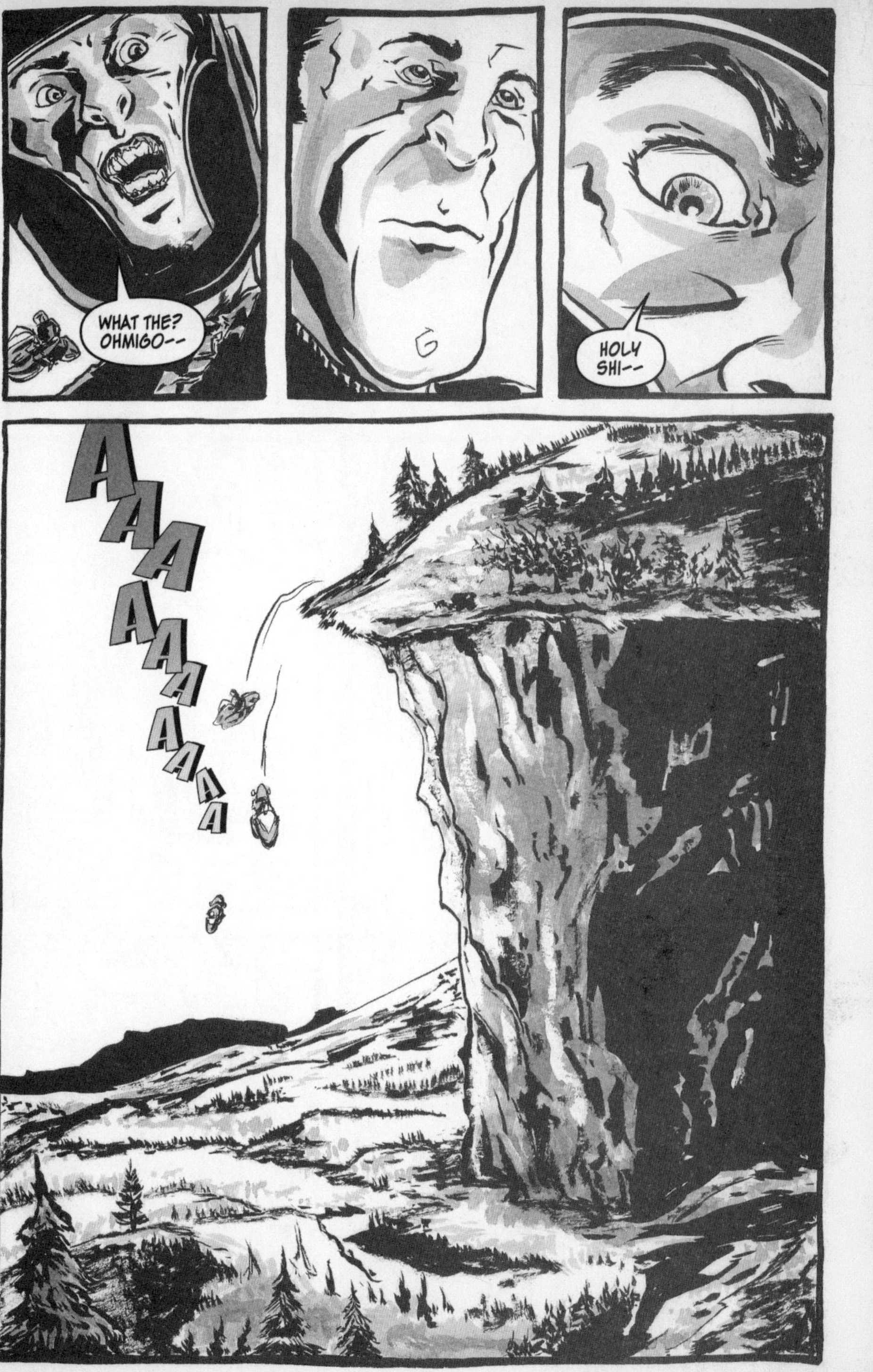
WHAT THE? OHMIGO--
G
HOLY SHI--
AAAAAAAAAAAA

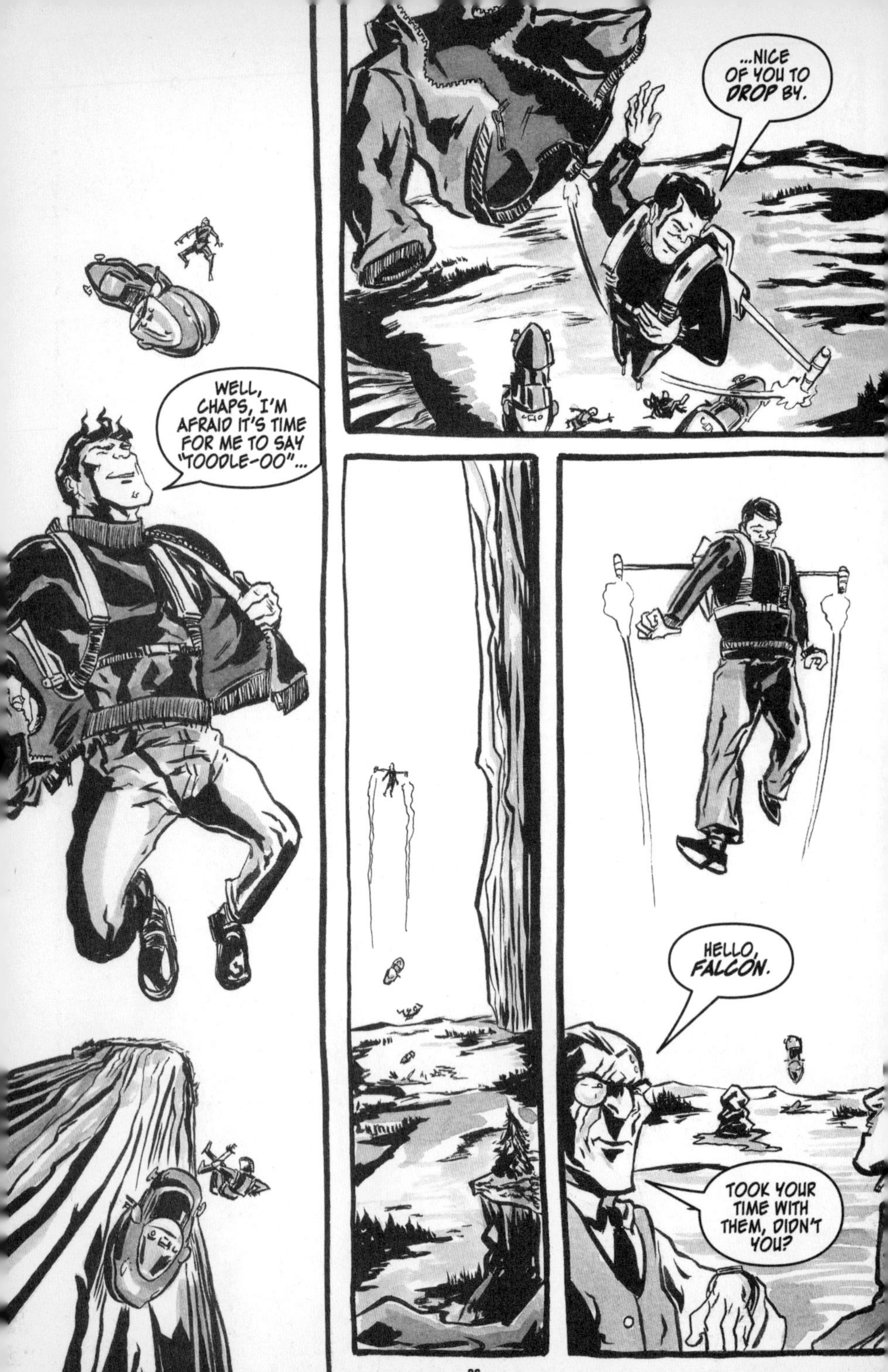
WELL, CHAPS, I'M AFRAID IT'S TIME FOR ME TO SAY "TOODLE-OO"...
...NICE OF YOU TO DROP BY.
HELLO, FALCON.
TOOK YOUR TIME WITH THEM, DIDN'T YOU?

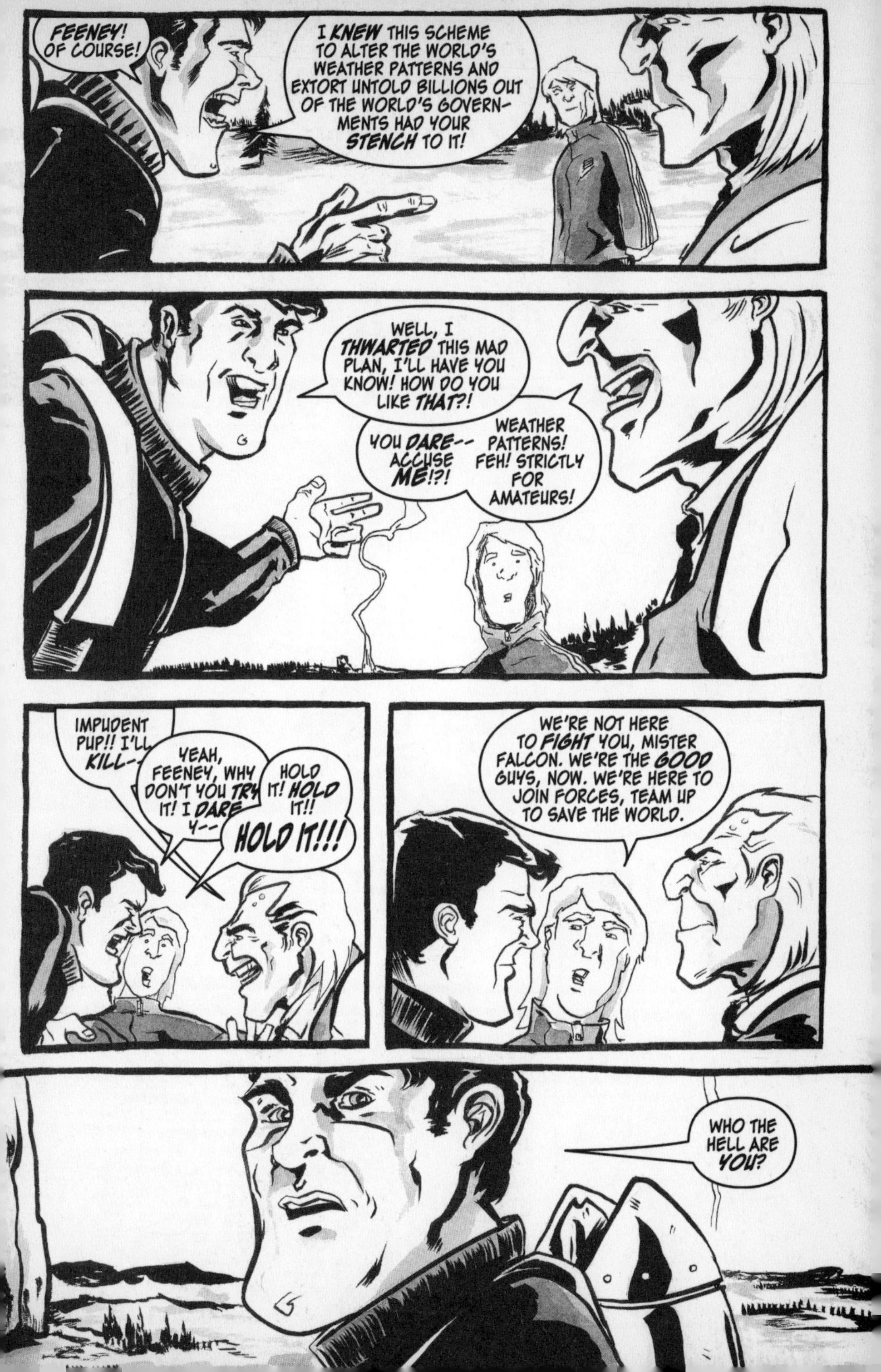
FEENEY! OF COURSE!
I KNEW THIS SCHEME TO ALTER THE WORLD'S WEATHER PATTERNS AND EXTORT UNTOLD BILLIONS OUT OF THE WORLD'S GOVERNMENTS HAD YOUR STENCH TO IT!
WELL, I THWARTED THIS MAD PLAN, I'LL HAVE YOU KNOW! HOW DO YOU LIKE THAT?!
YOU DARE-- ACCUSE ME!?!
WEATHER PATTERNS! FEH! STRICTLY FOR AMATEURS!
IMPUDENT PUP!! I'LL KILL--
YEAH, FEENEY, WHY DON'T YOU TRY IT! I DARE Y--
HOLD IT! HOLD IT!!
HOLD IT!!!
WE'RE NOT HERE TO FIGHT YOU, MISTER FALCON. WE'RE THE GOOD GUYS, NOW. WE'RE HERE TO JOIN FORCES, TEAM UP TO SAVE THE WORLD.
WHO THE HELL ARE YOU?

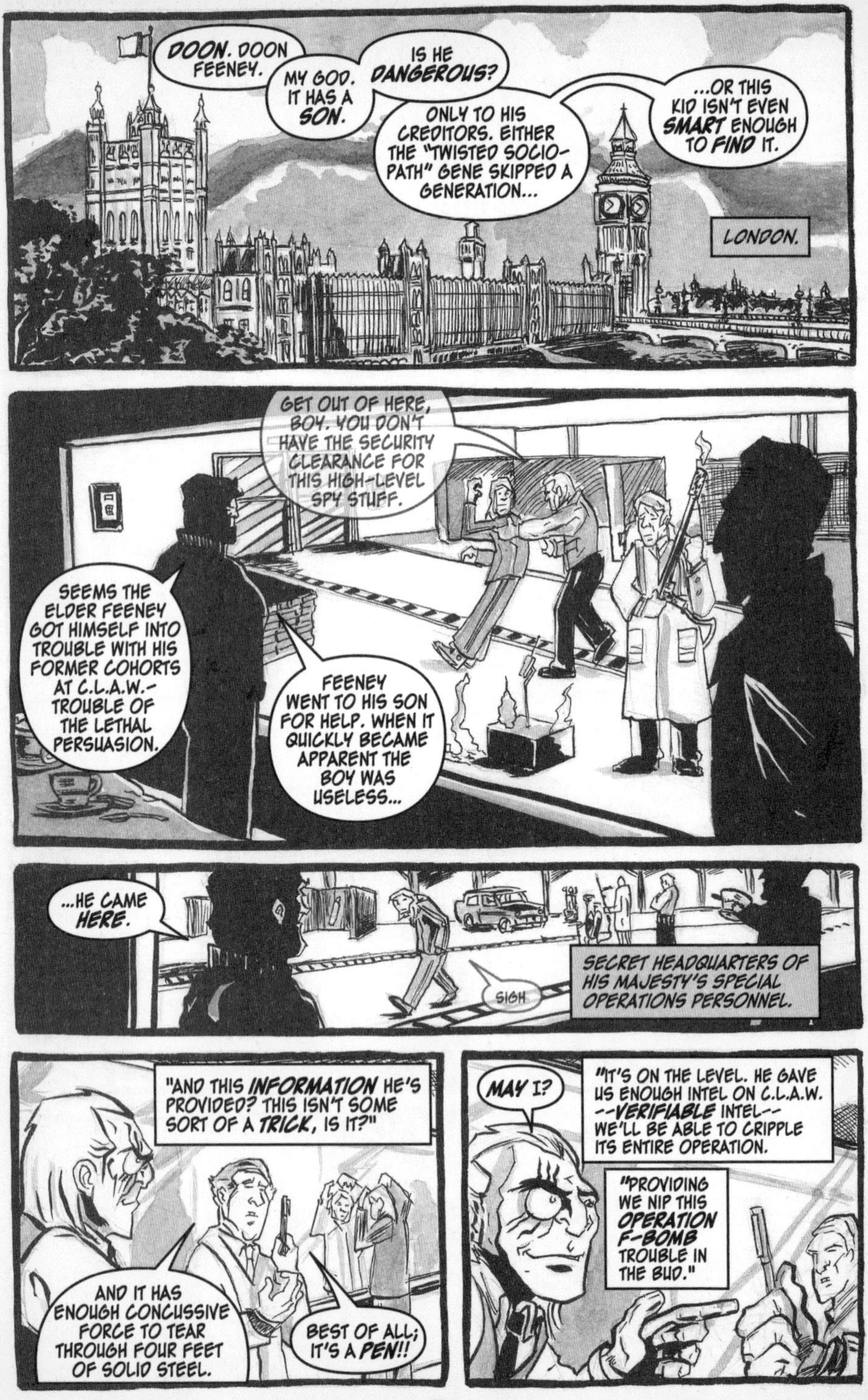
DOON. DOON FEENEY.
MY GOD. IT HAS A SON.
IS HE DANGEROUS?
ONLY TO HIS CREDITORS. EITHER THE "TWISTED SOCIO-PATH" GENE SKIPPED A GENERATION...
...OR THIS KID ISN'T EVEN SMART ENOUGH TO FIND IT.
LONDON.
GET OUT OF HERE, BOY. YOU DON'T HAVE THE SECURITY CLEARANCE FOR THIS HIGH-LEVEL SPY STUFF.
SEEMS THE ELDER FEENEY GOT HIMSELF INTO TROUBLE WITH HIS FORMER COHORTS AT C.L.A.W.- TROUBLE OF THE LETHAL PERSUASION.
FEENEY WENT TO HIS SON FOR HELP. WHEN IT QUICKLY BECAME APPARENT THE BOY WAS USELESS...
...HE CAME HERE.
SIGH
SECRET HEADQUARTERS OF HIS MAJESTY'S SPECIAL OPERATIONS PERSONNEL.
"AND THIS INFORMATION HE'S PROVIDED? THIS ISN'T SOME SORT OF A TRICK, IS IT?"
AND IT HAS ENOUGH CONCUSSIVE FORCE TO TEAR THROUGH FOUR FEET OF SOLID STEEL.
BEST OF ALL; IT'S A PEN!!
MAY I?
"IT'S ON THE LEVEL. HE GAVE US ENOUGH INTEL ON C.L.A.W. --VERIFIABLE INTEL-- WE'LL BE ABLE TO CRIPPLE ITS ENTIRE OPERATION.
"PROVIDING WE NIP THIS OPERATION F-BOMB TROUBLE IN THE BUD."

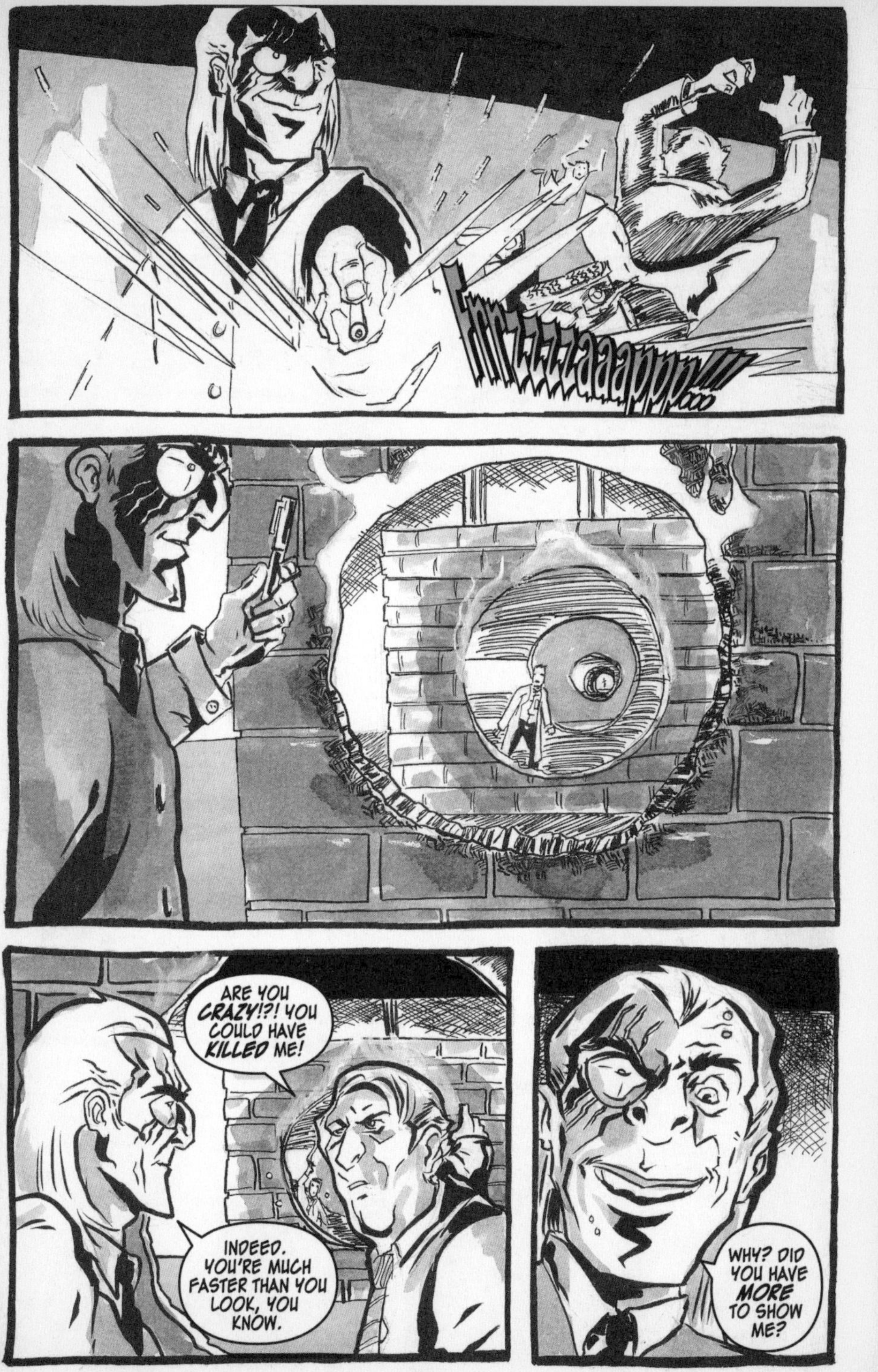
FRRZZZZZAAAPPP!!!
ARE YOU CRAZY!?! YOU COULD HAVE KILLED ME!
INDEED. YOU'RE MUCH FASTER THAN YOU LOOK, YOU KNOW.
WHY? DID YOU HAVE MORE TO SHOW ME?

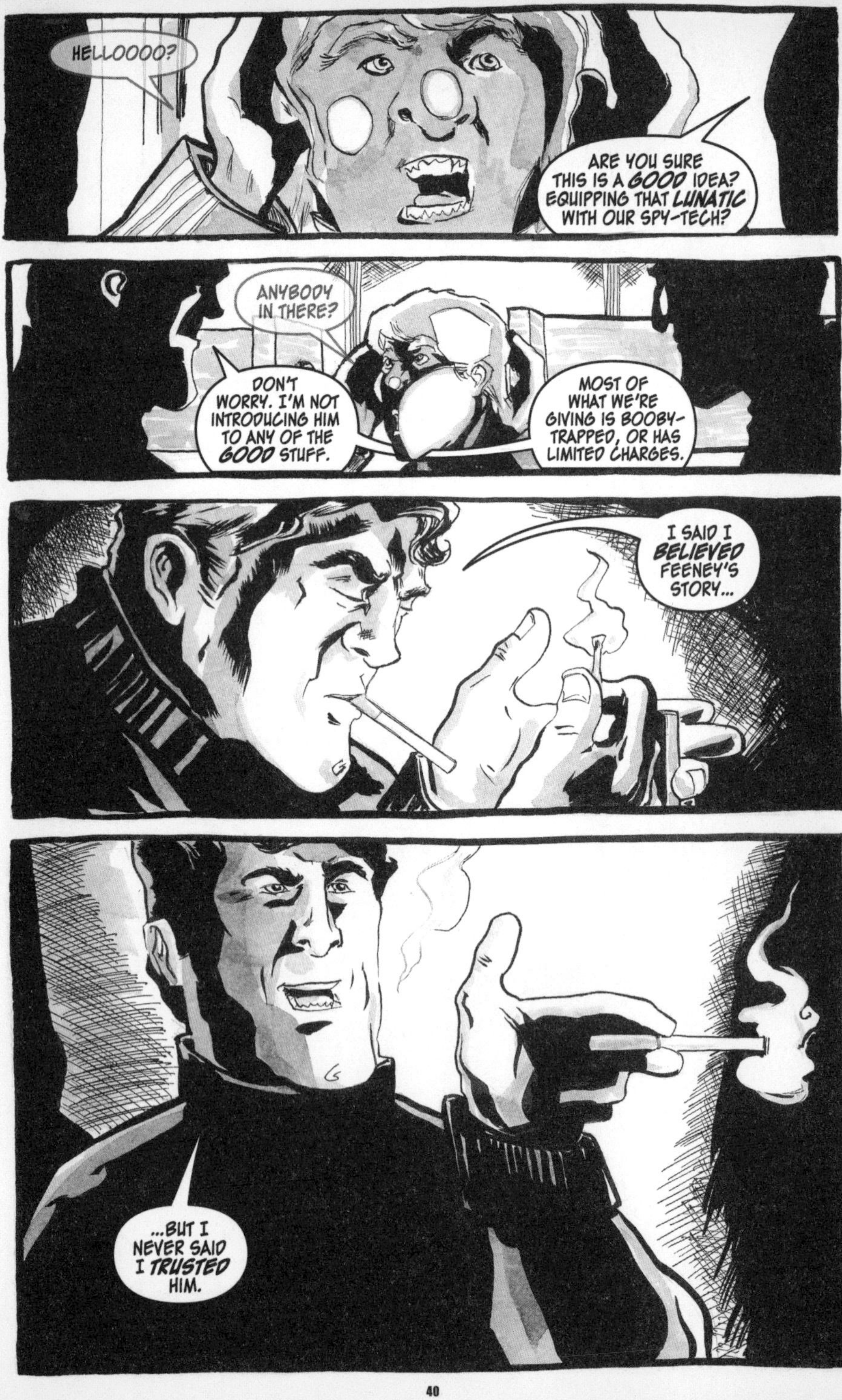
HELLOOOO?
ARE YOU SURE THIS IS A GOOD IDEA? EQUIPPING THAT LUNATIC WITH OUR SPY-TECH?
ANYBODY IN THERE?
DON'T WORRY. I'M NOT INTRODUCING HIM TO ANY OF THE GOOD STUFF.
MOST OF WHAT WE'RE GIVING IS BOOBY-TRAPPED, OR HAS LIMITED CHARGES.
I SAID I BELIEVED FEENEY'S STORY...
...BUT I NEVER SAID I TRUSTED HIM.

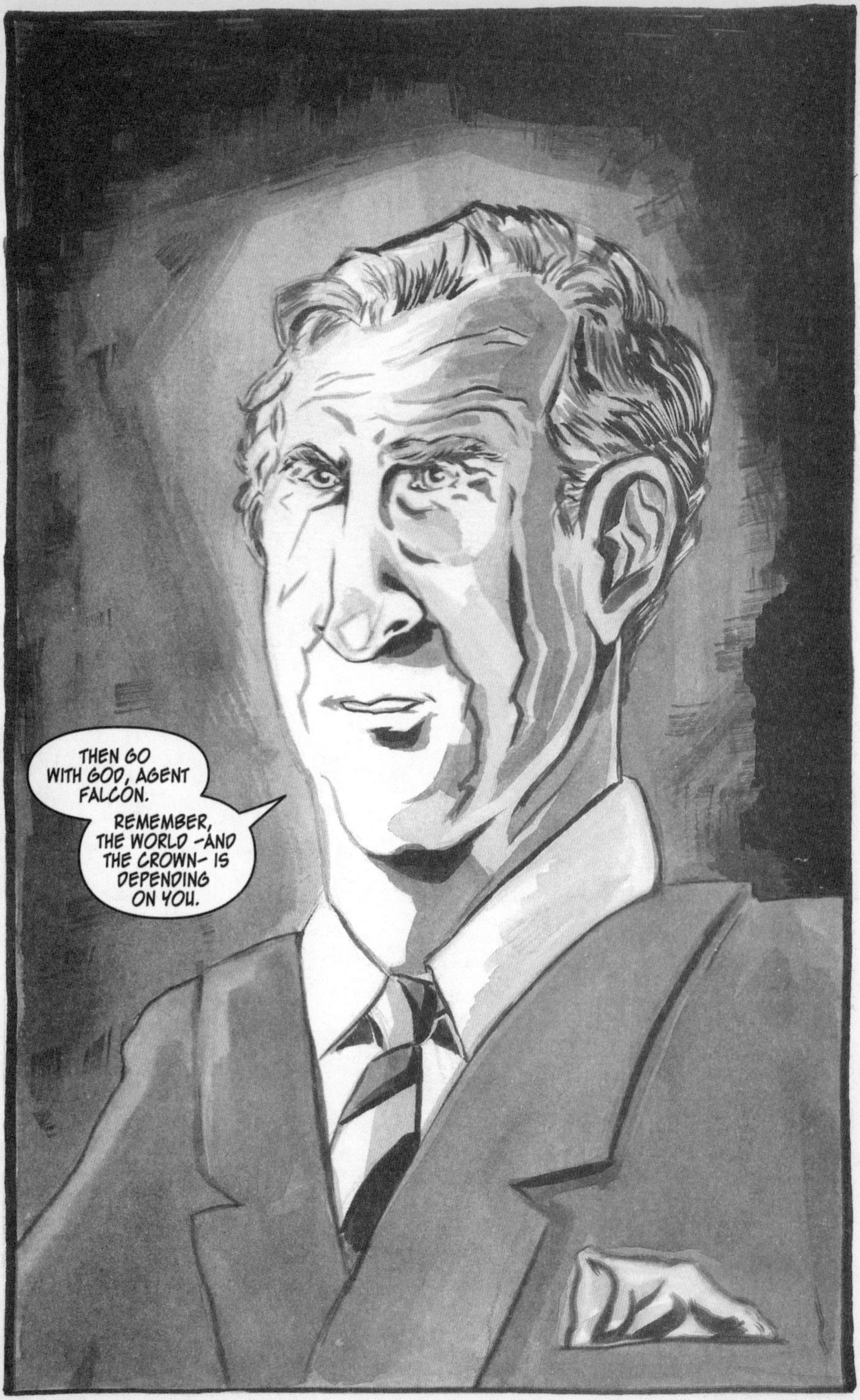
THEN GO WITH GOD, AGENT FALCON.
REMEMBER, THE WORLD -AND THE CROWN- IS DEPENDING ON YOU.

AFTER DINNER.

FUNNY, ISN'T IT, FEENEY? AFTER ALL THE YEARS WE SPENT TRYING TO KILL EACH OTHER, FINALLY TEAMING UP TO SAVE THE WORLD. WHO WOULD HAVE GUESSED!?

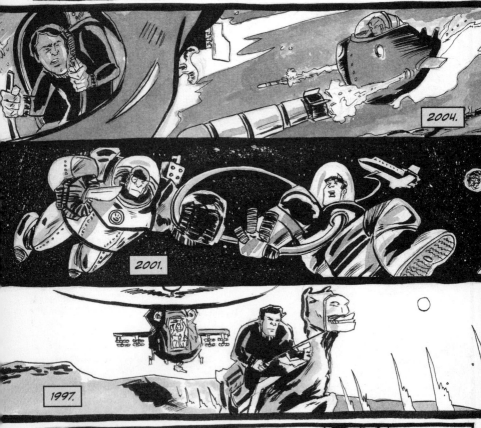

2004.

2001.

1997.

HRRM.

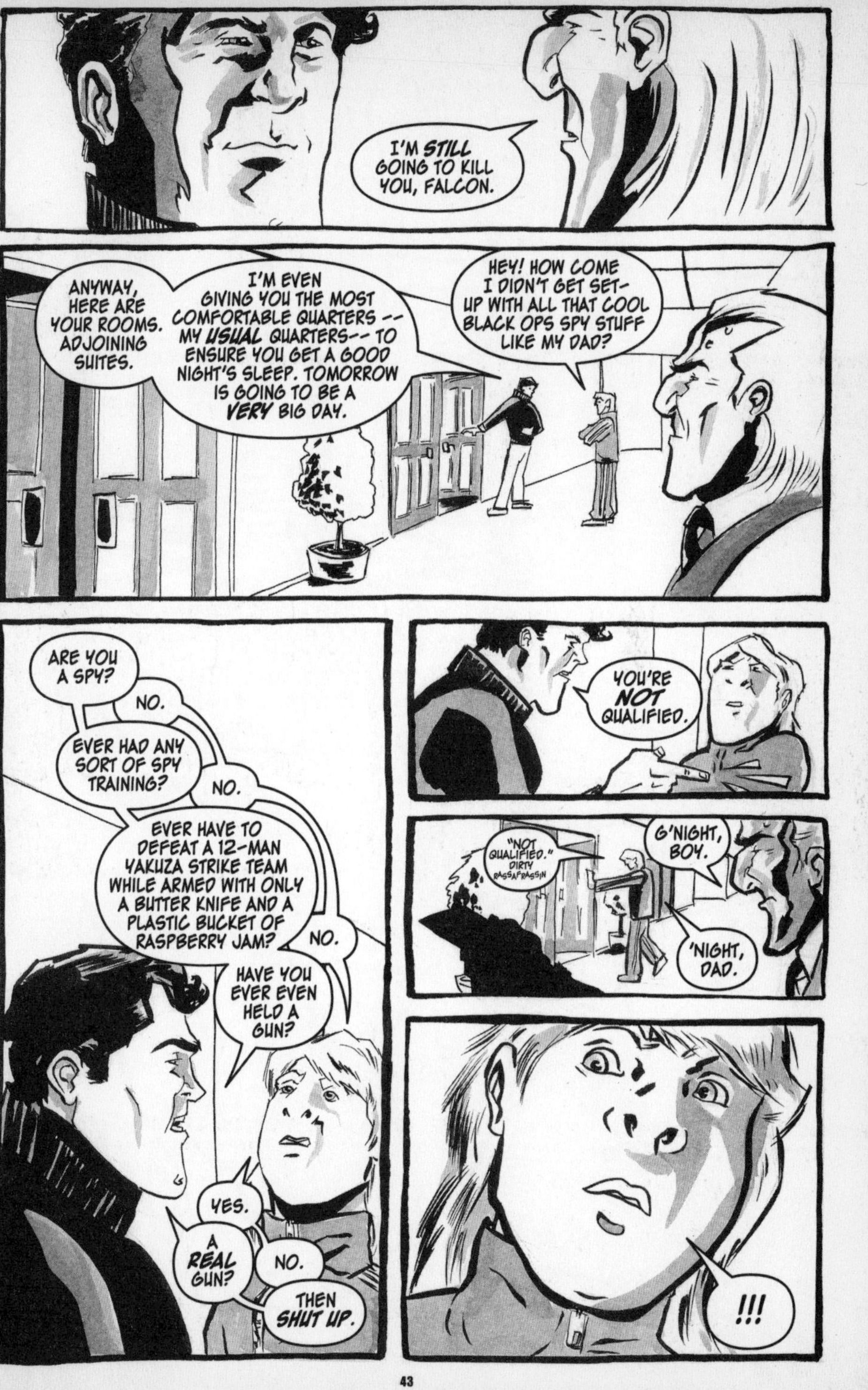

I'M STILL GOING TO KILL YOU, FALCON.
ANYWAY, HERE ARE YOUR ROOMS. ADJOINING SUITES.
I'M EVEN GIVING YOU THE MOST COMFORTABLE QUARTERS -- MY USUAL QUARTERS-- TO ENSURE YOU GET A GOOD NIGHT'S SLEEP. TOMORROW IS GOING TO BE A VERY BIG DAY.
HEY! HOW COME I DIDN'T GET SET-UP WITH ALL THAT COOL BLACK OPS SPY STUFF LIKE MY DAD?
ARE YOU A SPY?
NO.
EVER HAD ANY SORT OF SPY TRAINING?
NO.
EVER HAVE TO DEFEAT A 12-MAN YAKUZA STRIKE TEAM WHILE ARMED WITH ONLY A BUTTER KNIFE AND A PLASTIC BUCKET OF RASPBERRY JAM?
NO.
HAVE YOU EVER EVEN HELD A GUN?
YES.
A REAL GUN?
NO.
THEN SHUT UP.
YOU'RE NOT QUALIFIED.
G'NIGHT, BOY.
'NIGHT, DAD.
"NOT QUALIFIED." DIRTY RASSAFRASSIN
!!!

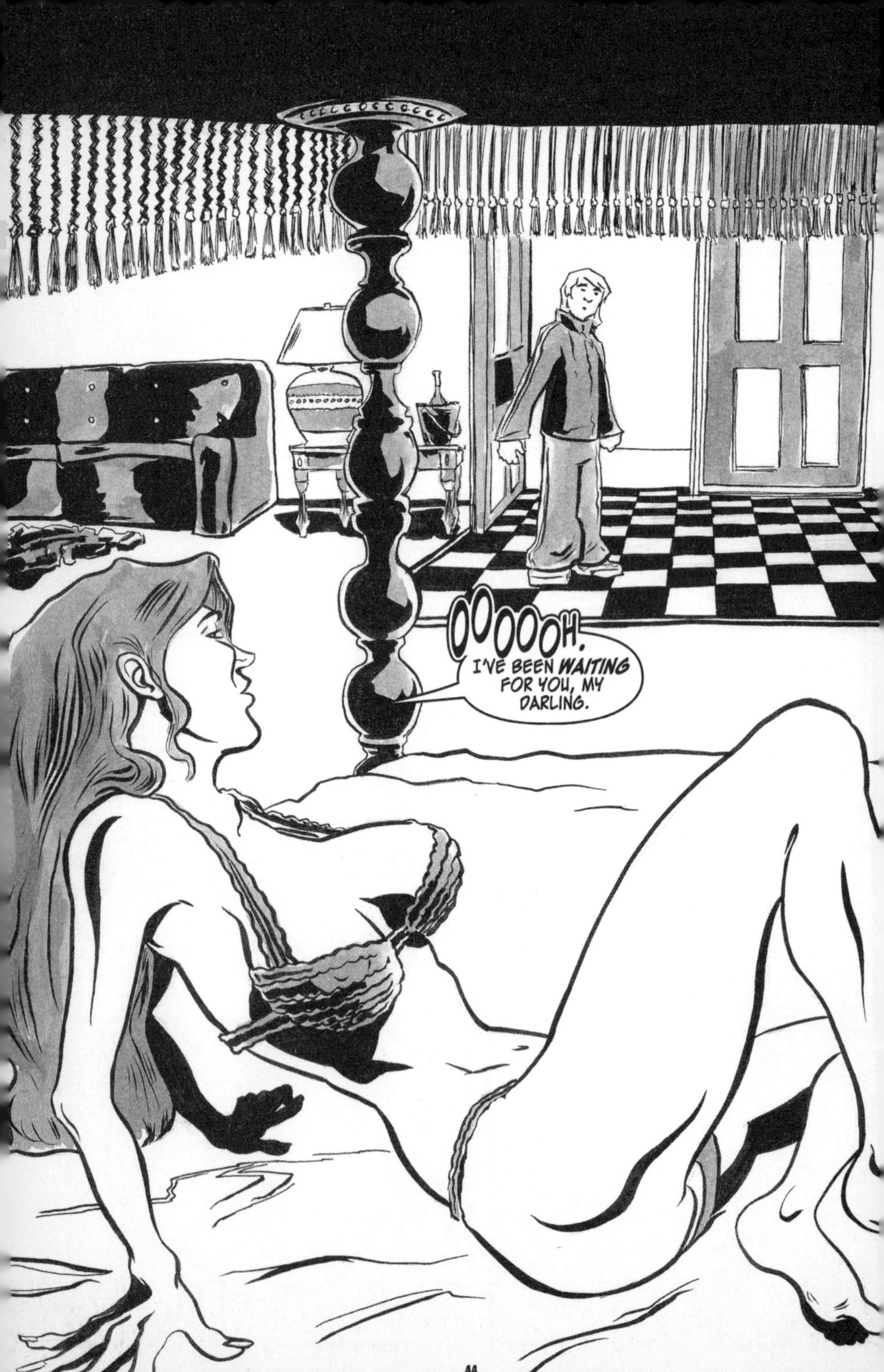
OOOOOH.
I'VE BEEN **WAITING** FOR YOU, MY DARLING.

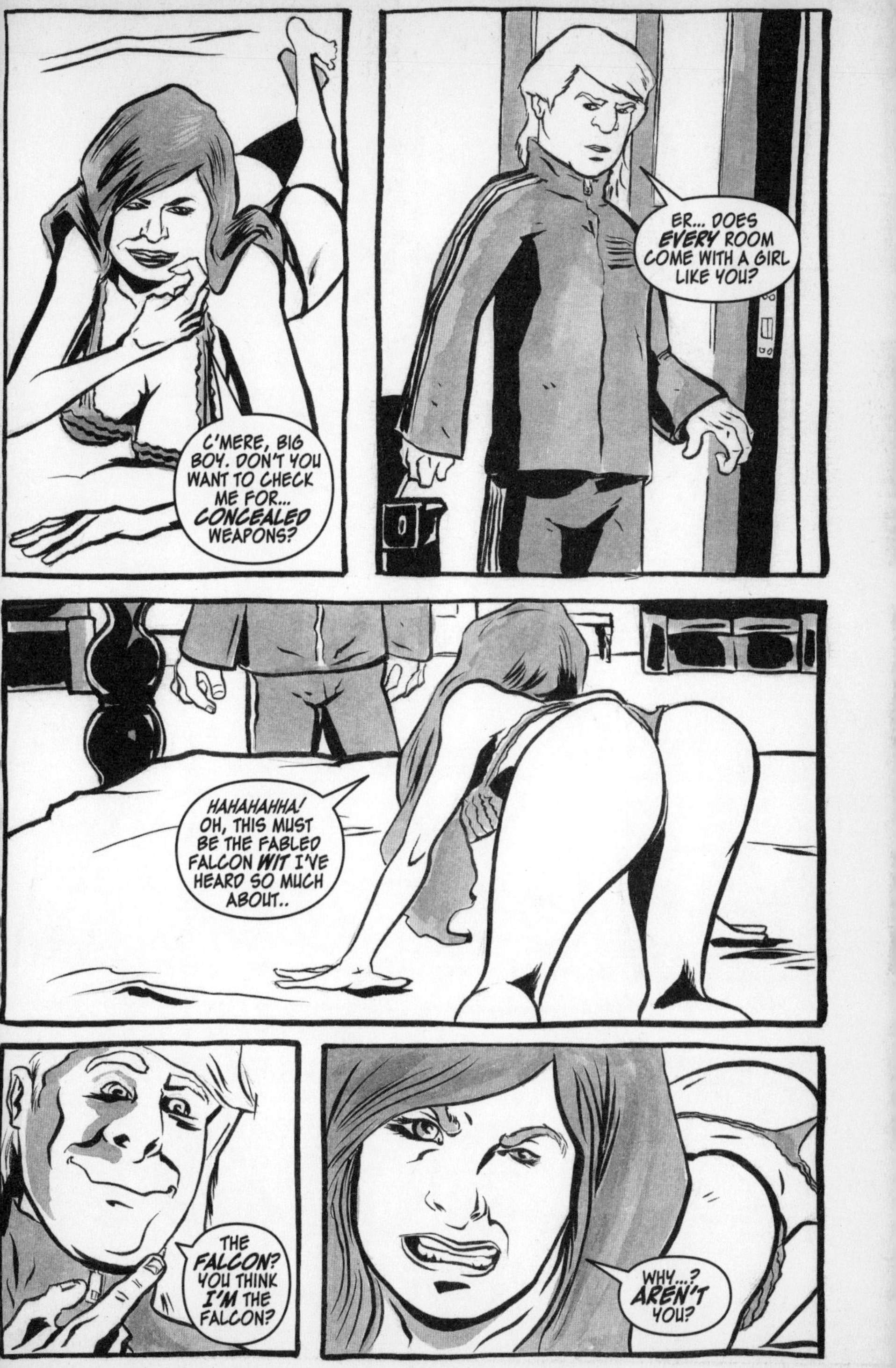
C'MERE, BIG BOY. DON'T YOU WANT TO CHECK ME FOR... CONCEALED WEAPONS?
ER... DOES EVERY ROOM COME WITH A GIRL LIKE YOU?
HAHAHAHHA! OH, THIS MUST BE THE FABLED FALCON WIT I'VE HEARD SO MUCH ABOUT..
THE FALCON? YOU THINK I'M THE FALCON?
WHY...? AREN'T YOU?

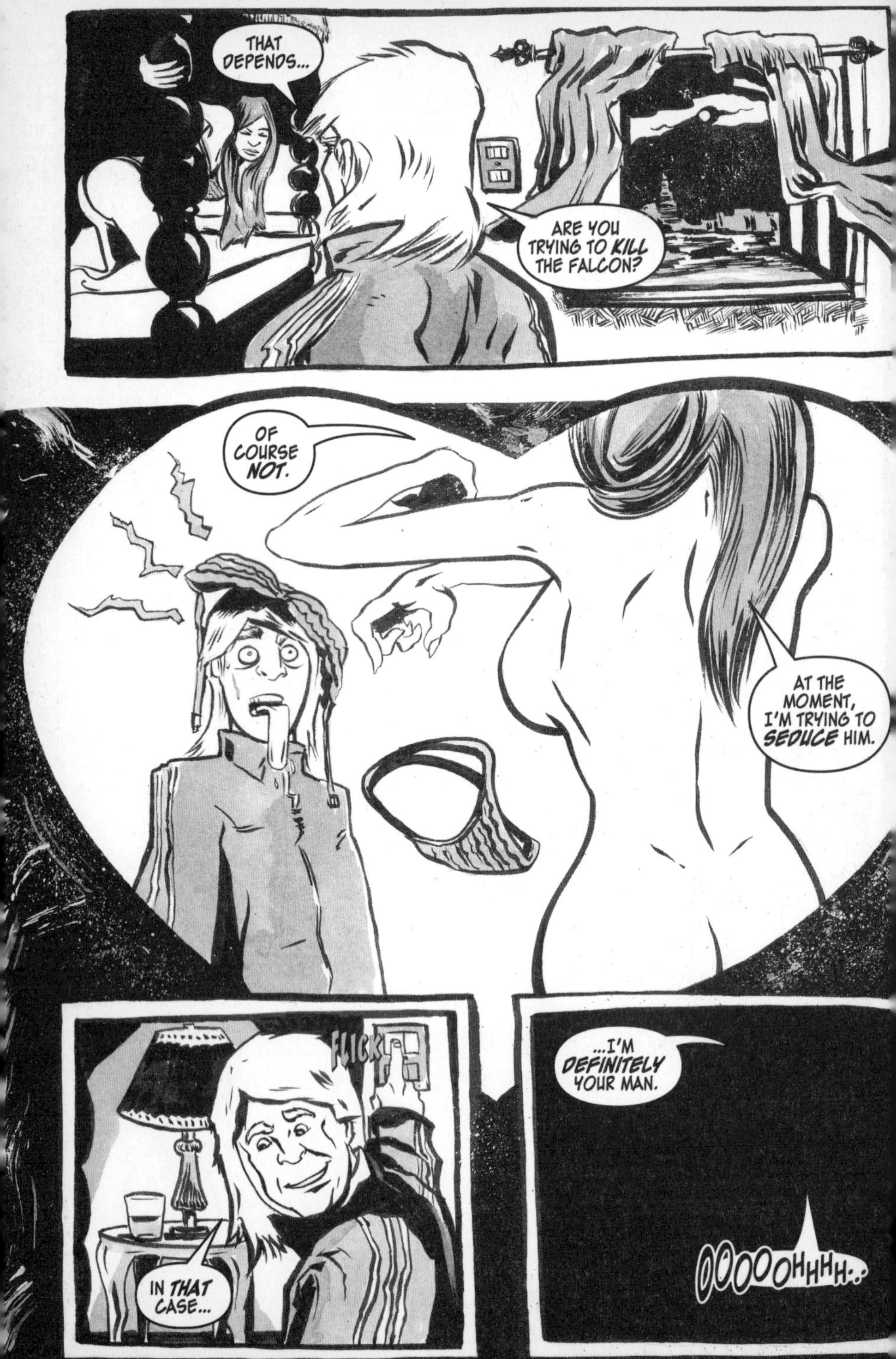
THAT DEPENDS...
ARE YOU TRYING TO KILL THE FALCON?
OF COURSE NOT.
AT THE MOMENT, I'M TRYING TO SEDUCE HIM.
FLICK
IN THAT CASE...
...I'M DEFINITELY YOUR MAN.
OOOOOHHHH..

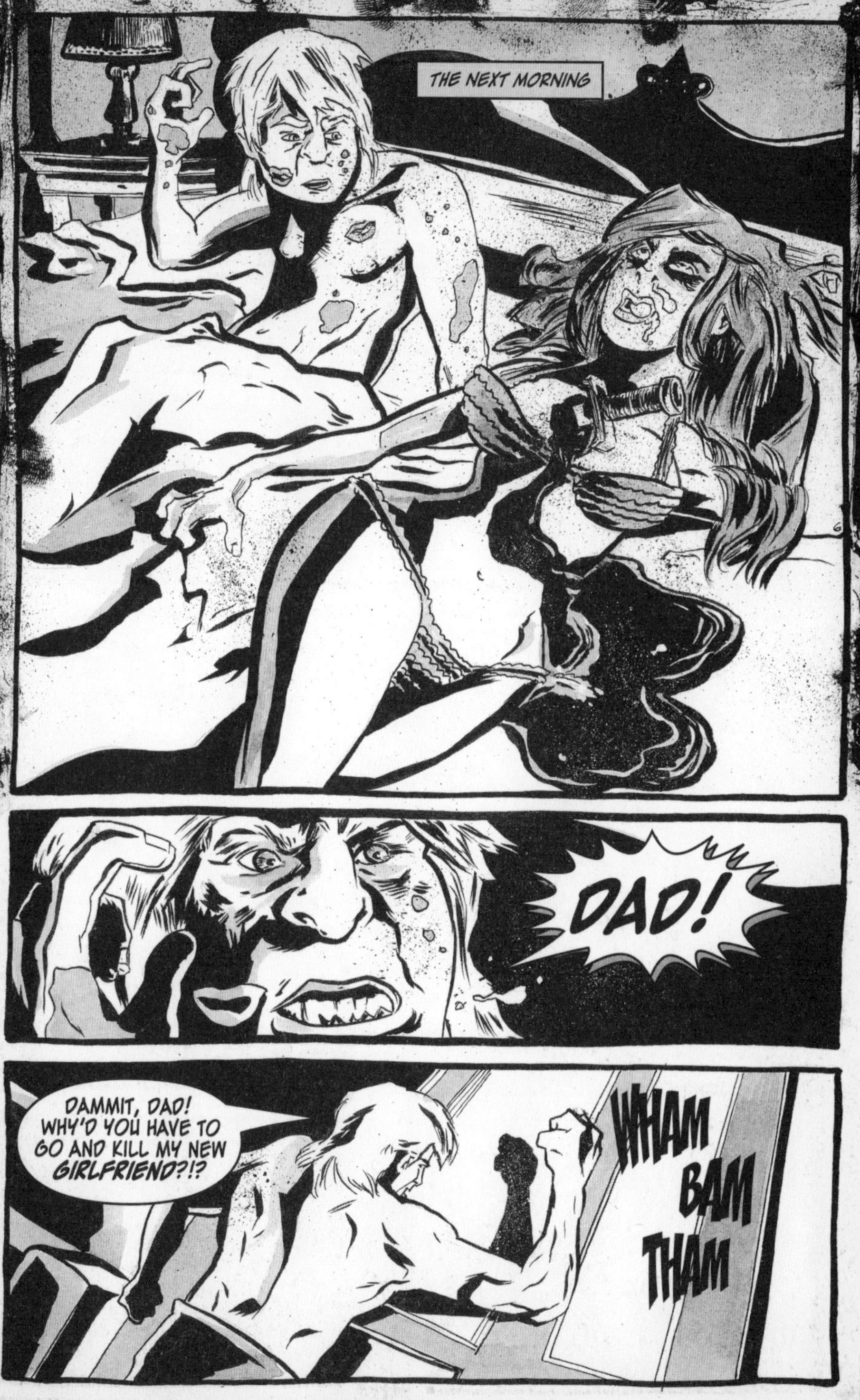
THE NEXT MORNING
DAD!
DAMMIT, DAD! WHY'D YOU HAVE TO GO AND KILL MY NEW GIRLFRIEND?!?
WHAM
BAM
THAM

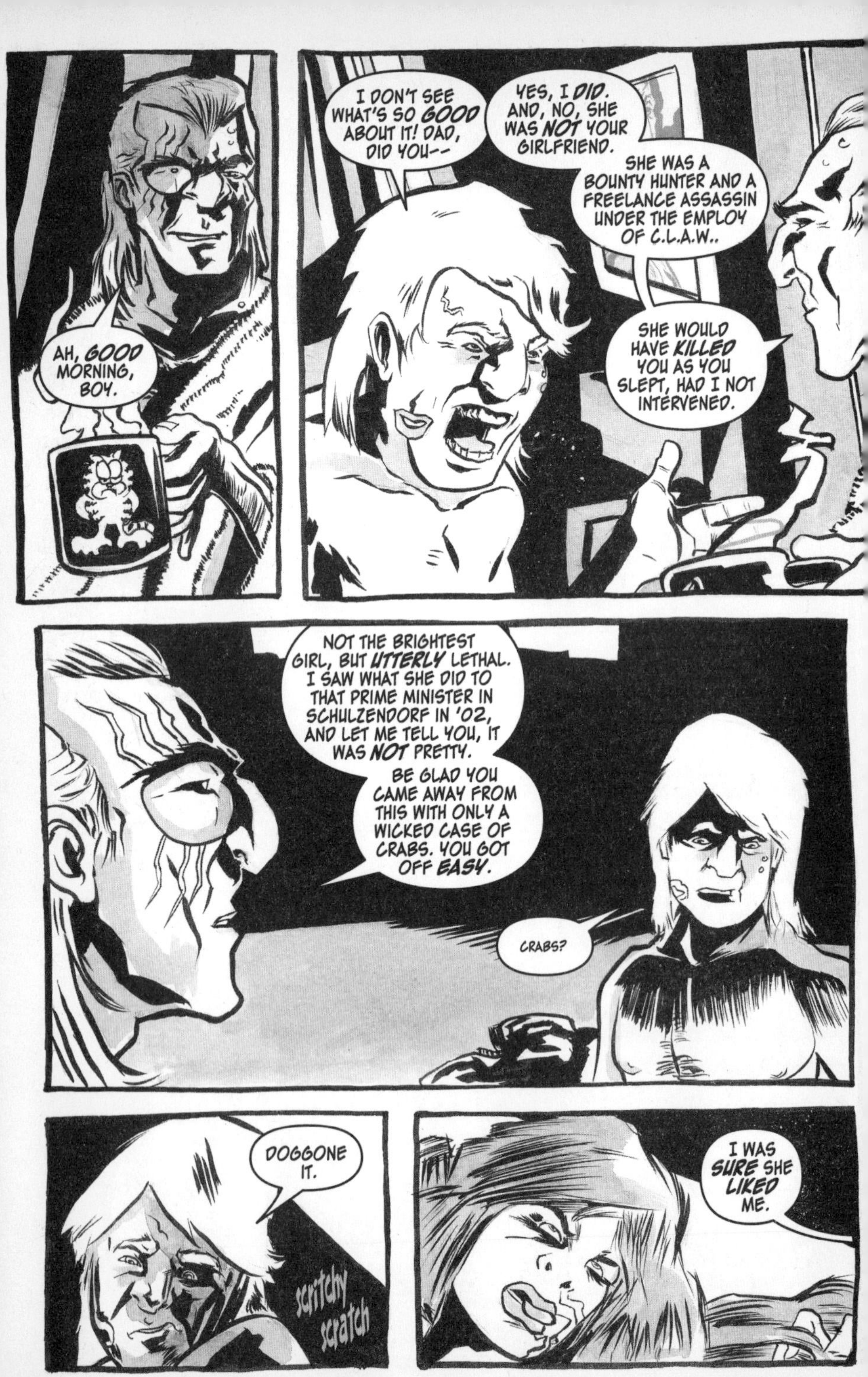

AH, GOOD MORNING, BOY.
I DON'T SEE WHAT'S SO GOOD ABOUT IT! DAD, DID YOU--
YES, I DID. AND, NO, SHE WAS NOT YOUR GIRLFRIEND.
SHE WAS A BOUNTY HUNTER AND A FREELANCE ASSASSIN UNDER THE EMPLOY OF C.L.A.W..
SHE WOULD HAVE KILLED YOU AS YOU SLEPT, HAD I NOT INTERVENED.
NOT THE BRIGHTEST GIRL, BUT UTTERLY LETHAL. I SAW WHAT SHE DID TO THAT PRIME MINISTER IN SCHULZENDORF IN '02, AND LET ME TELL YOU, IT WAS NOT PRETTY.
BE GLAD YOU CAME AWAY FROM THIS WITH ONLY A WICKED CASE OF CRABS. YOU GOT OFF EASY.
CRABS?
DOGGONE IT.
scritchy scratch
I WAS SURE SHE LIKED ME.

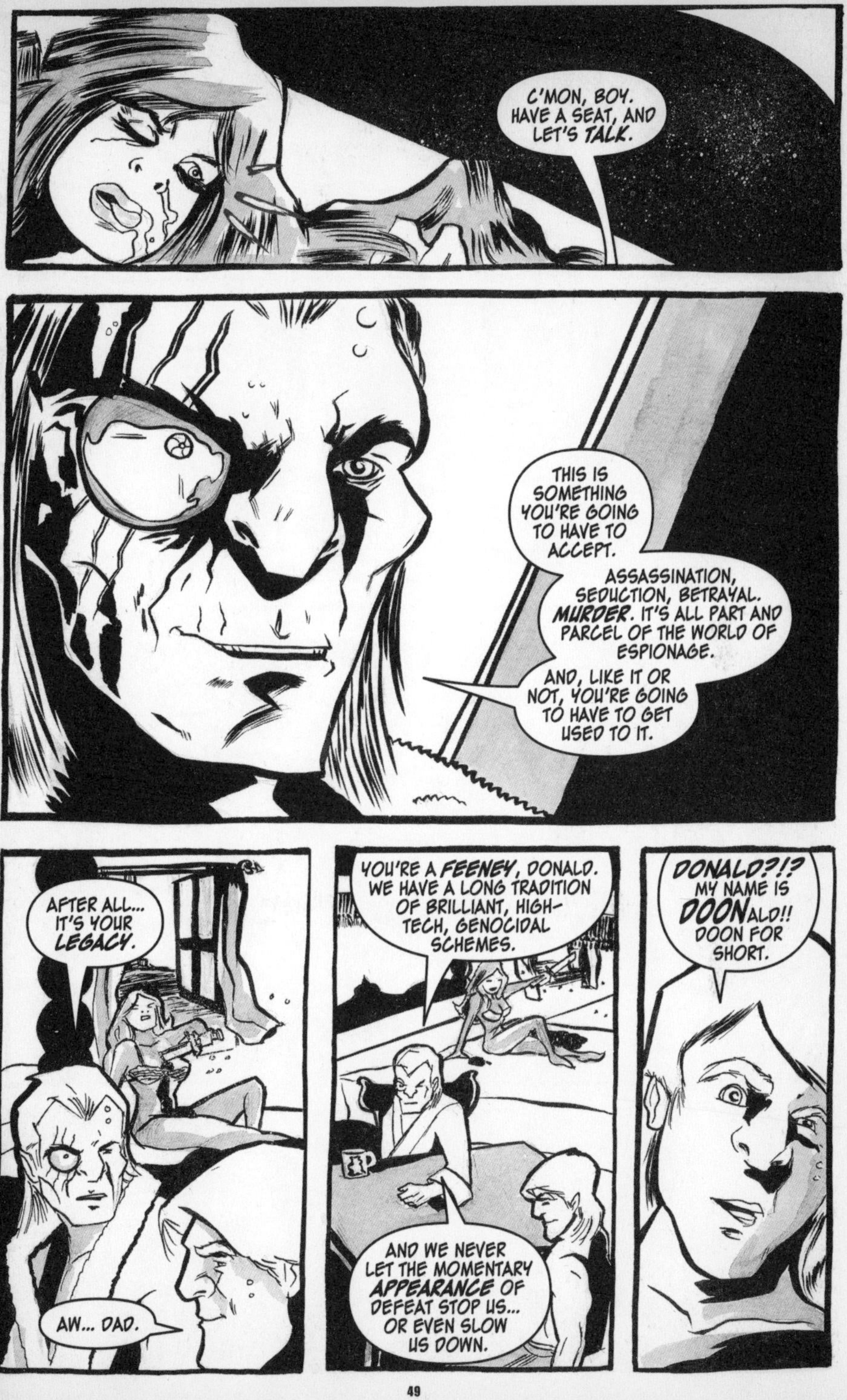
C'MON, BOY. HAVE A SEAT, AND LET'S TALK.
THIS IS SOMETHING YOU'RE GOING TO HAVE TO ACCEPT.
ASSASSINATION, SEDUCTION, BETRAYAL. MURDER. IT'S ALL PART AND PARCEL OF THE WORLD OF ESPIONAGE.
AND, LIKE IT OR NOT, YOU'RE GOING TO HAVE TO GET USED TO IT.
AFTER ALL... IT'S YOUR LEGACY.
AW... DAD.
YOU'RE A FEENEY, DONALD. WE HAVE A LONG TRADITION OF BRILLIANT, HIGH-TECH, GENOCIDAL SCHEMES.
AND WE NEVER LET THE MOMENTARY APPEARANCE OF DEFEAT STOP US... OR EVEN SLOW US DOWN.
DONALD?!? MY NAME IS DOONALD!! DOON FOR SHORT.

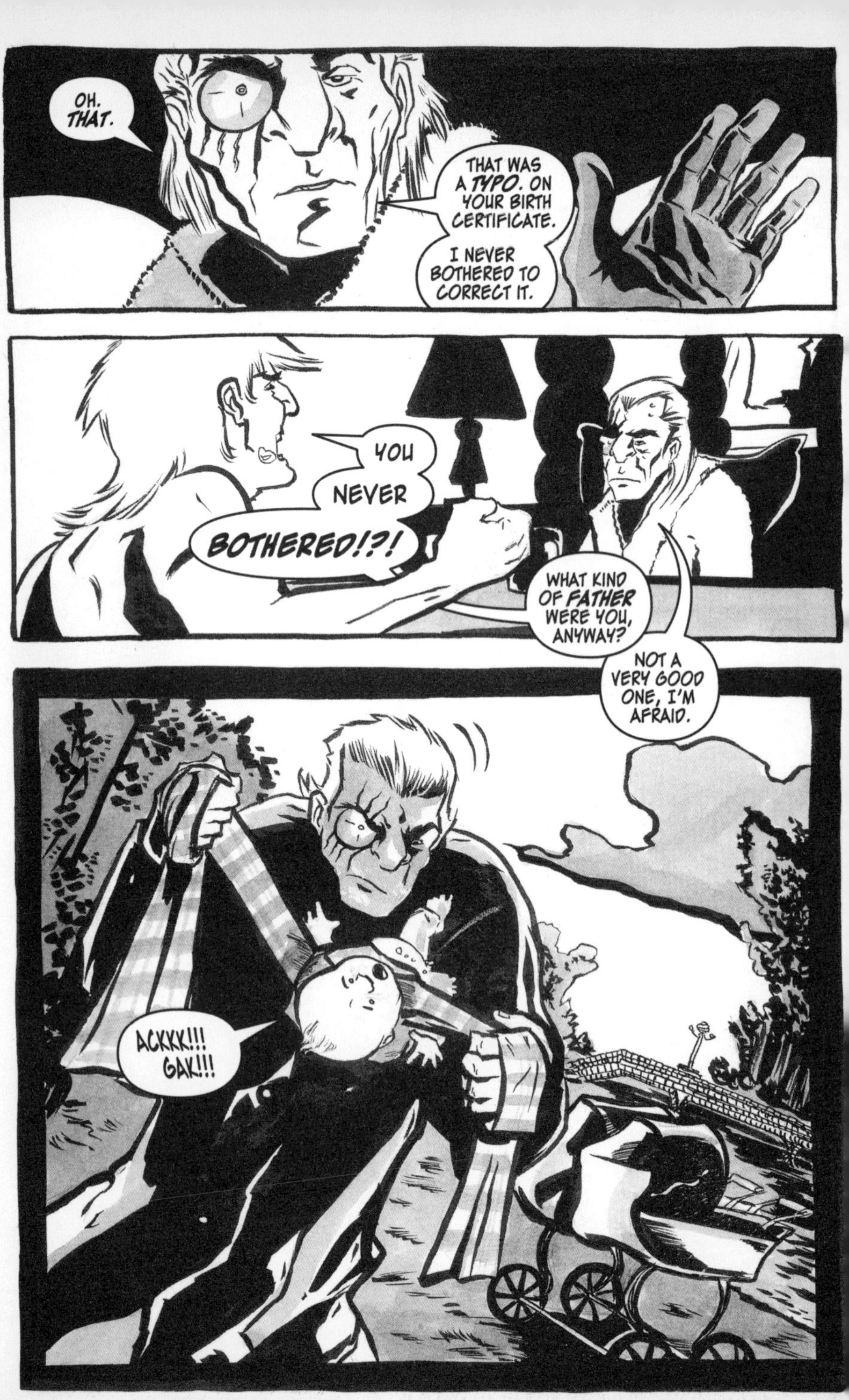
OH. THAT.
THAT WAS A TYPO. ON YOUR BIRTH CERTIFICATE.
I NEVER BOTHERED TO CORRECT IT.
YOU NEVER BOTHERED!?!
WHAT KIND OF FATHER WERE YOU, ANYWAY?
NOT A VERY GOOD ONE, I'M AFRAID.
ACKKK!!! GAK!!!

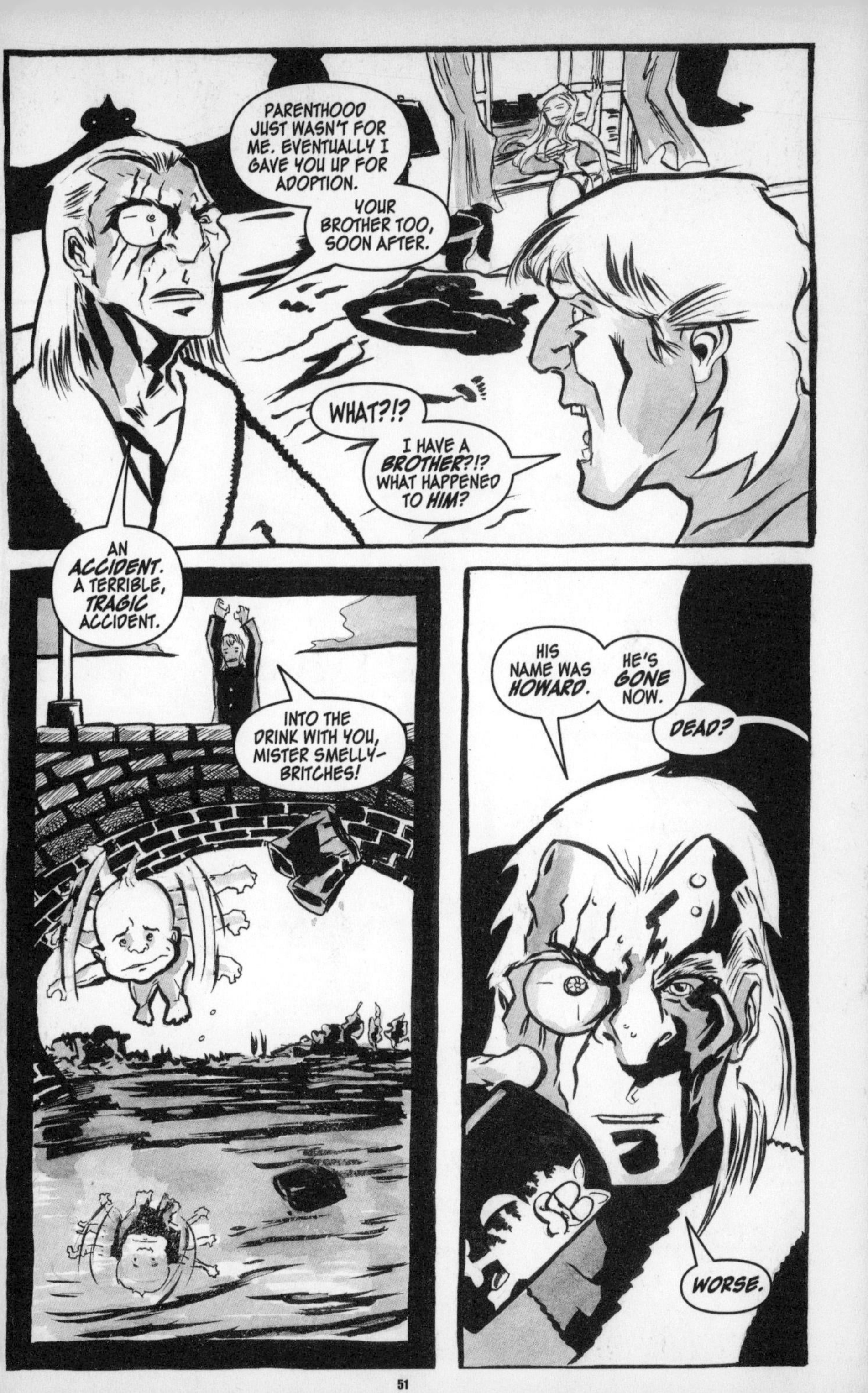
PARENTHOOD JUST WASN'T FOR ME. EVENTUALLY I GAVE YOU UP FOR ADOPTION.
YOUR BROTHER TOO, SOON AFTER.
WHAT?!?
I HAVE A BROTHER?!? WHAT HAPPENED TO HIM?
AN ACCIDENT. A TERRIBLE, TRAGIC ACCIDENT.
INTO THE DRINK WITH YOU, MISTER SMELLY-BRITCHES!
HIS NAME WAS HOWARD.
HE'S GONE NOW.
DEAD?
WORSE.

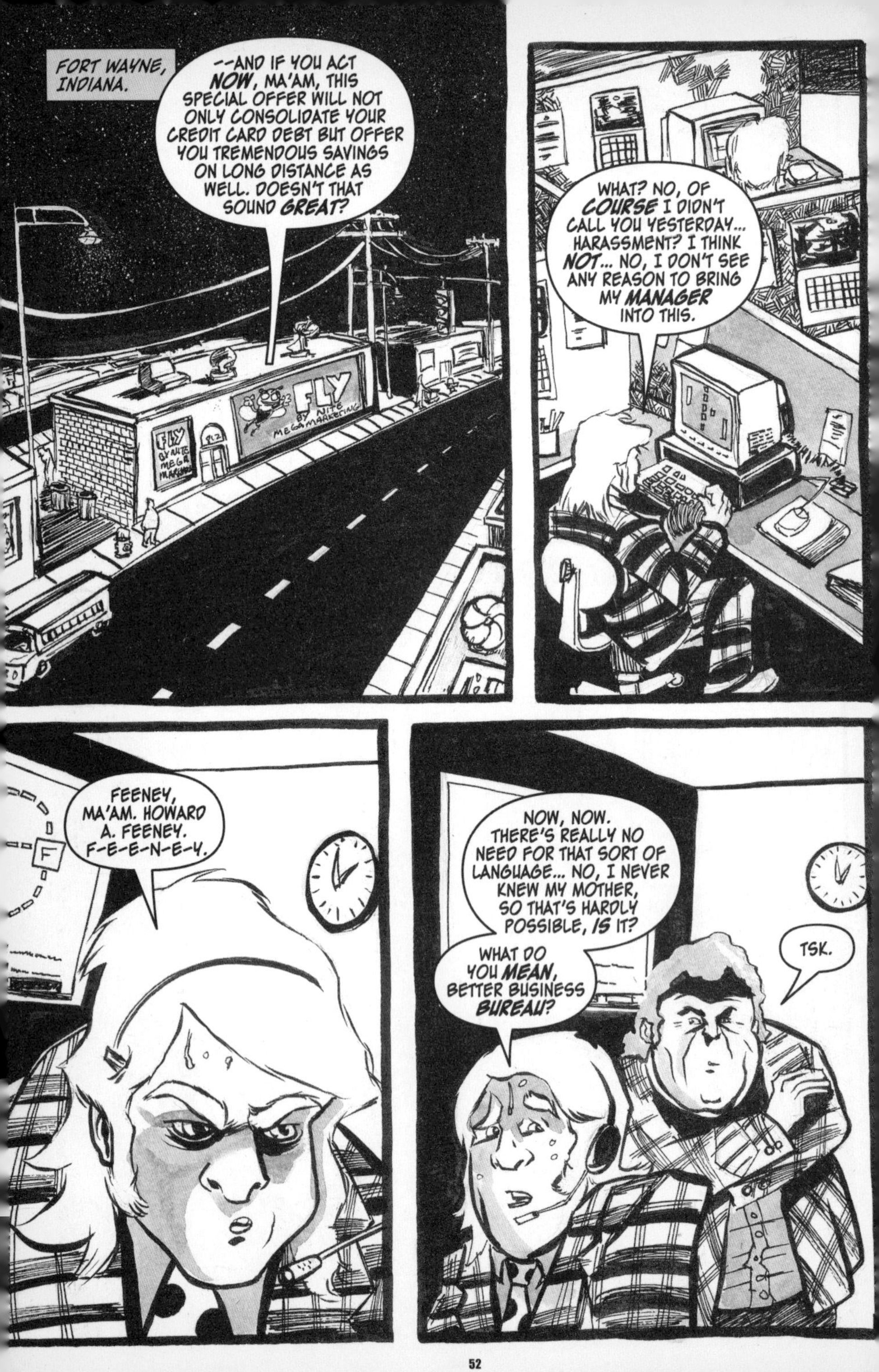
FORT WAYNE, INDIANA.
--AND IF YOU ACT NOW, MA'AM, THIS SPECIAL OFFER WILL NOT ONLY CONSOLIDATE YOUR CREDIT CARD DEBT BUT OFFER YOU TREMENDOUS SAVINGS ON LONG DISTANCE AS WELL. DOESN'T THAT SOUND GREAT?
FLY BY NITE MEGAMARKETING
WHAT? NO, OF COURSE I DIDN'T CALL YOU YESTERDAY... HARASSMENT? I THINK NOT... NO, I DON'T SEE ANY REASON TO BRING MY MANAGER INTO THIS.
FEENEY, MA'AM. HOWARD A. FEENEY. F-E-E-N-E-Y.
NOW, NOW. THERE'S REALLY NO NEED FOR THAT SORT OF LANGUAGE... NO, I NEVER KNEW MY MOTHER, SO THAT'S HARDLY POSSIBLE, IS IT?
WHAT DO YOU MEAN, BETTER BUSINESS BUREAU?
TSK.

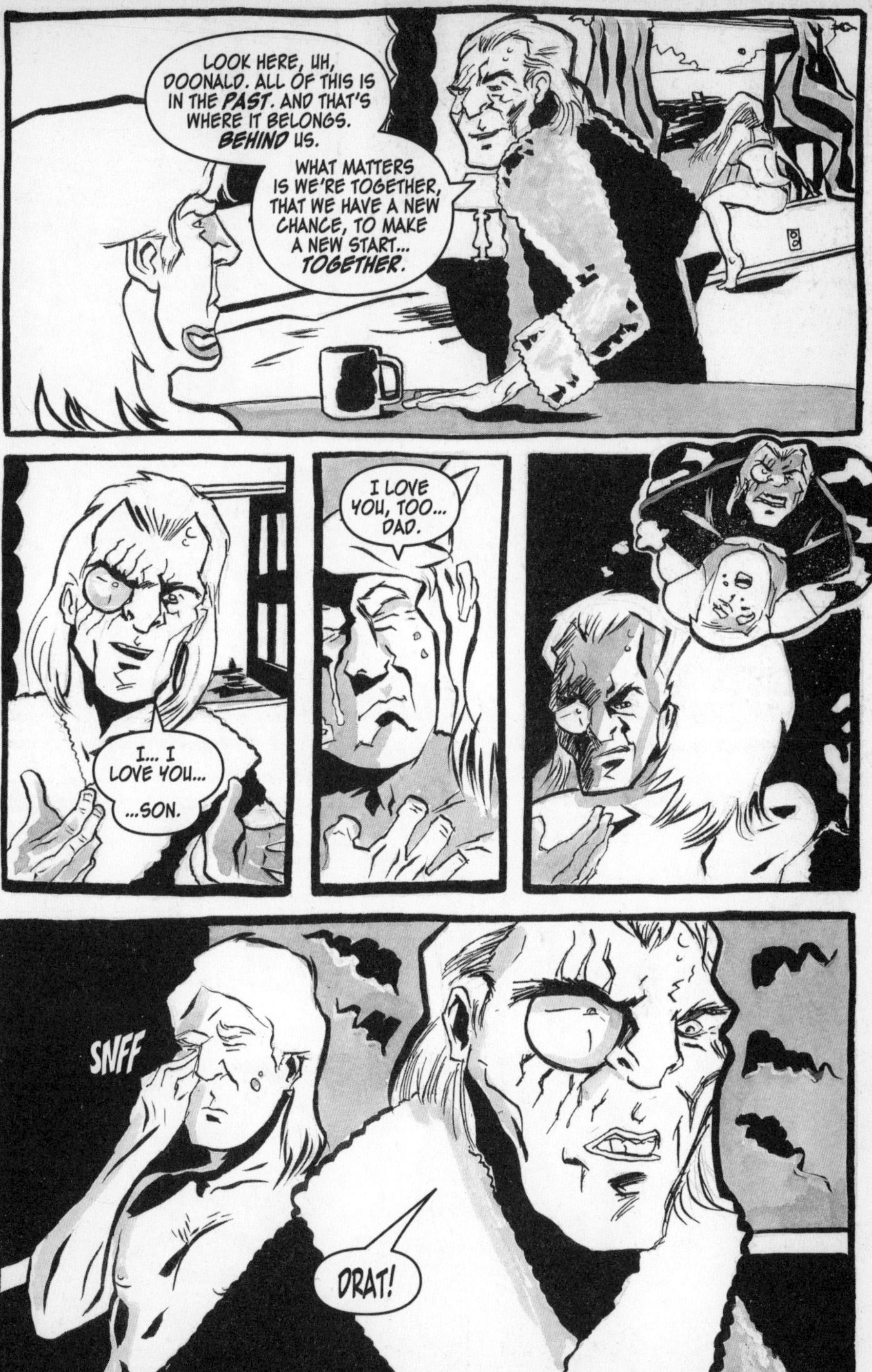
LOOK HERE, UH, DOONALD. ALL OF THIS IS IN THE PAST. AND THAT'S WHERE IT BELONGS. BEHIND US.
WHAT MATTERS IS WE'RE TOGETHER, THAT WE HAVE A NEW CHANCE, TO MAKE A NEW START... TOGETHER.
I... I LOVE YOU... ...SON.
I LOVE YOU, TOO... DAD.
SNFF
DRAT!

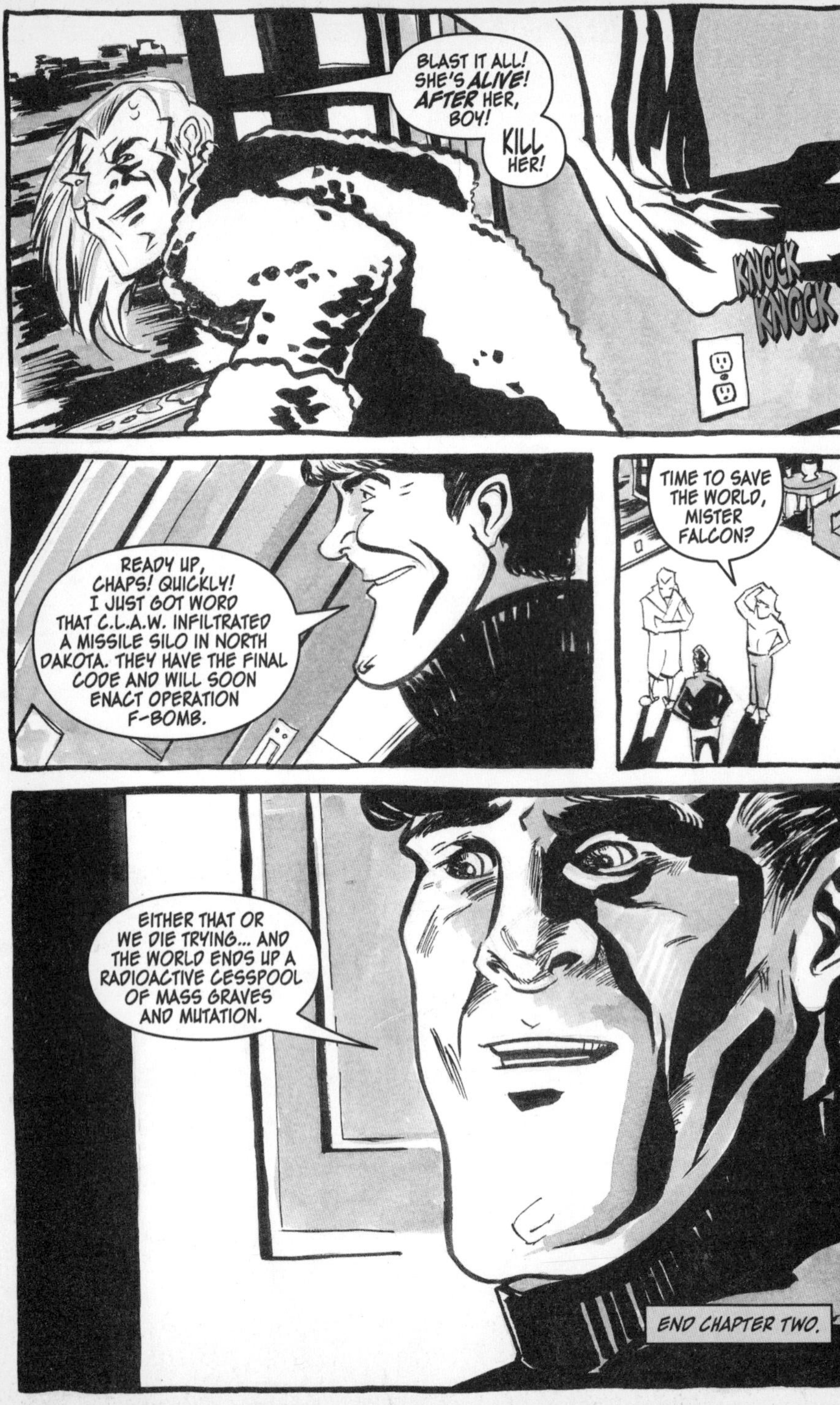

BLAST IT ALL! SHE'S ALIVE! AFTER HER, BOY!
KILL HER!
KNOCK KNOCK
READY UP, CHAPS! QUICKLY! I JUST GOT WORD THAT C.L.A.W. INFILTRATED A MISSILE SILO IN NORTH DAKOTA. THEY HAVE THE FINAL CODE AND WILL SOON ENACT OPERATION F-BOMB.
TIME TO SAVE THE WORLD, MISTER FALCON?
EITHER THAT OR WE DIE TRYING... AND THE WORLD ENDS UP A RADIOACTIVE CESSPOOL OF MASS GRAVES AND MUTATION.
END CHAPTER TWO.

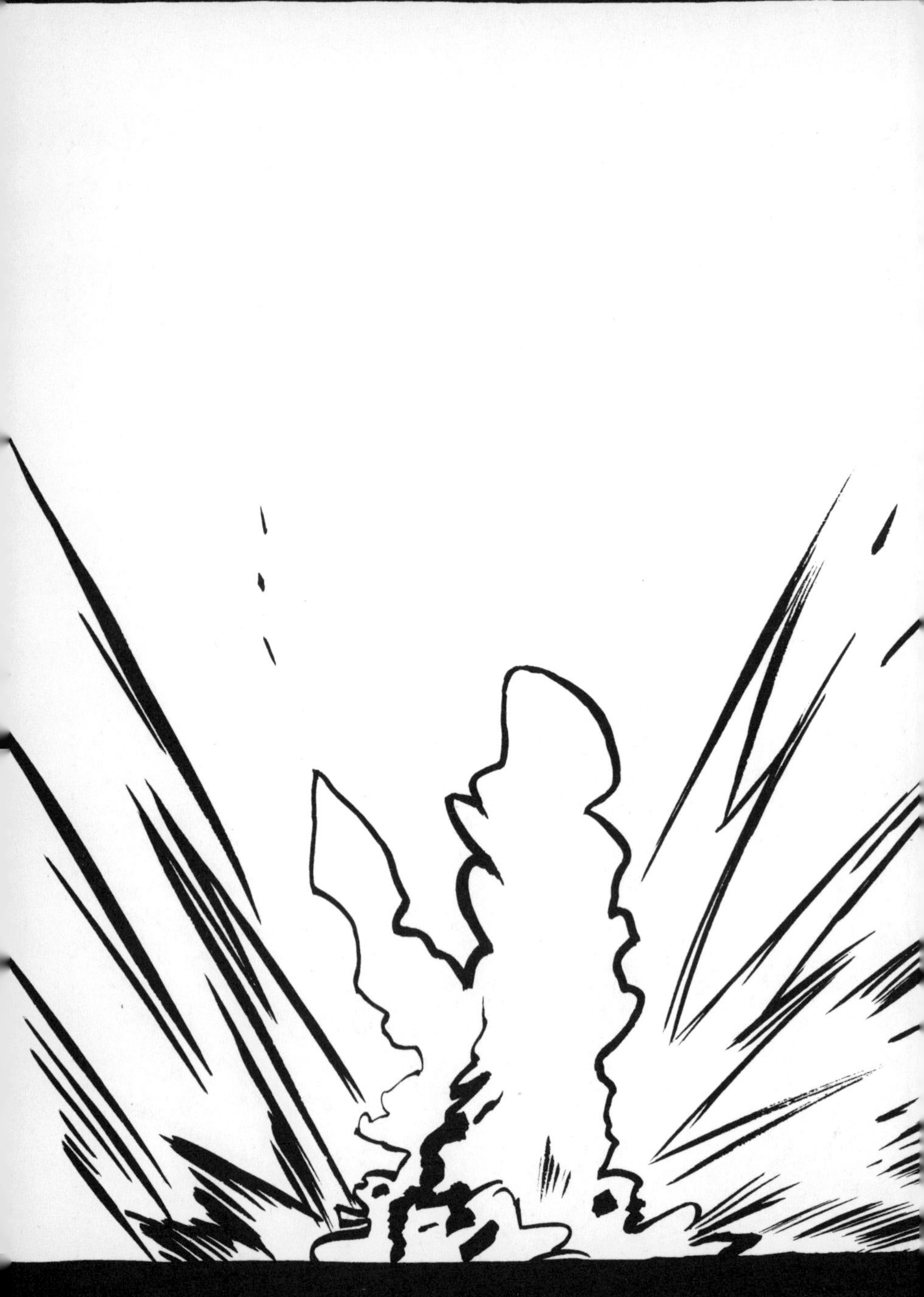

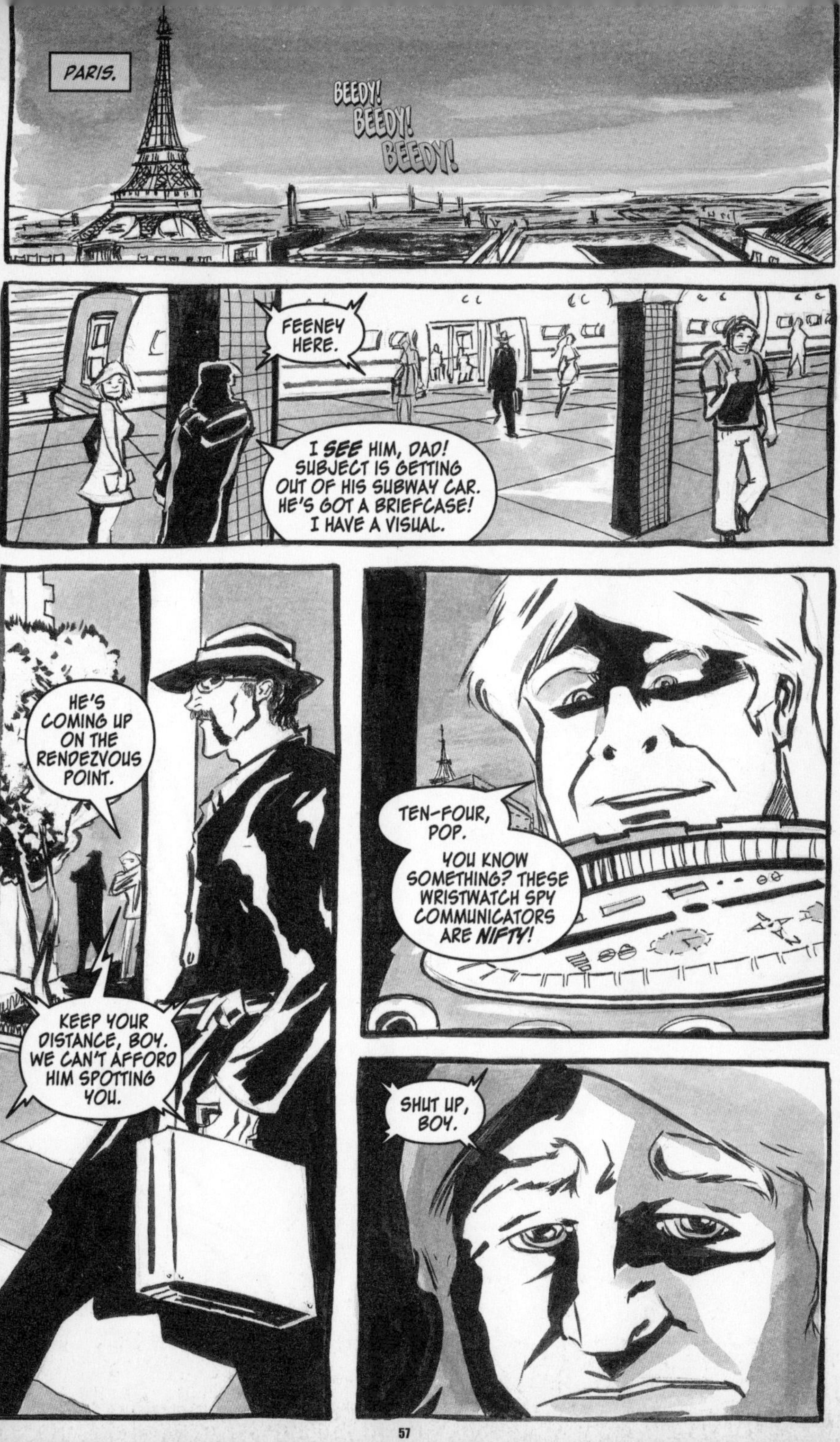

PARIS.
BEEDY! BEEDY! BEEDY!
FEENEY HERE.
I SEE HIM, DAD! SUBJECT IS GETTING OUT OF HIS SUBWAY CAR. HE'S GOT A BRIEFCASE! I HAVE A VISUAL.
HE'S COMING UP ON THE RENDEZVOUS POINT.
KEEP YOUR DISTANCE, BOY. WE CAN'T AFFORD HIM SPOTTING YOU.
TEN-FOUR, POP.
YOU KNOW SOMETHING? THESE WRISTWATCH SPY COMMUNICATORS ARE NIFTY!
SHUT UP, BOY.

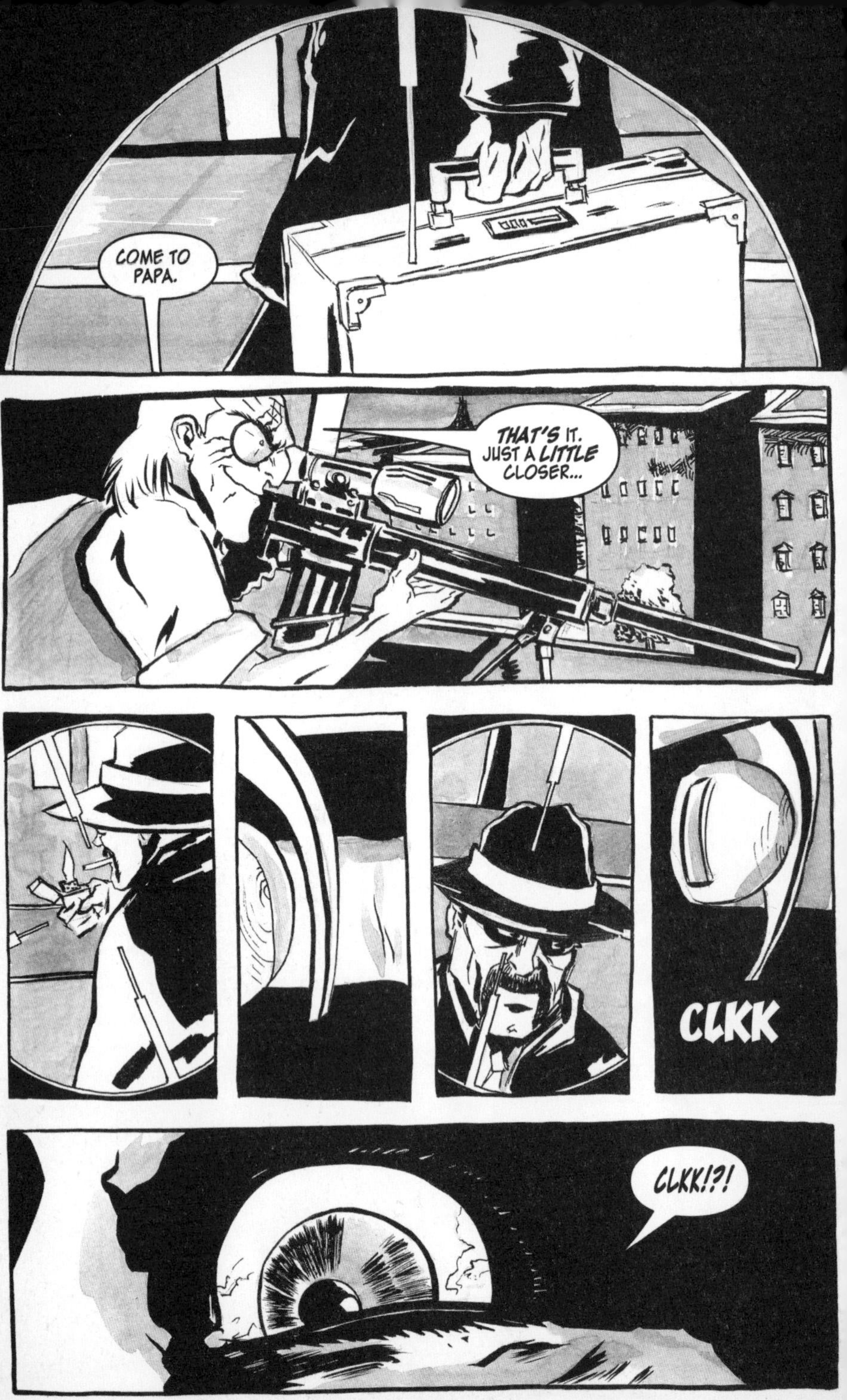
COME TO PAPA.
THAT'S IT. JUST A LITTLE CLOSER...
CLKK
CLKK!?!

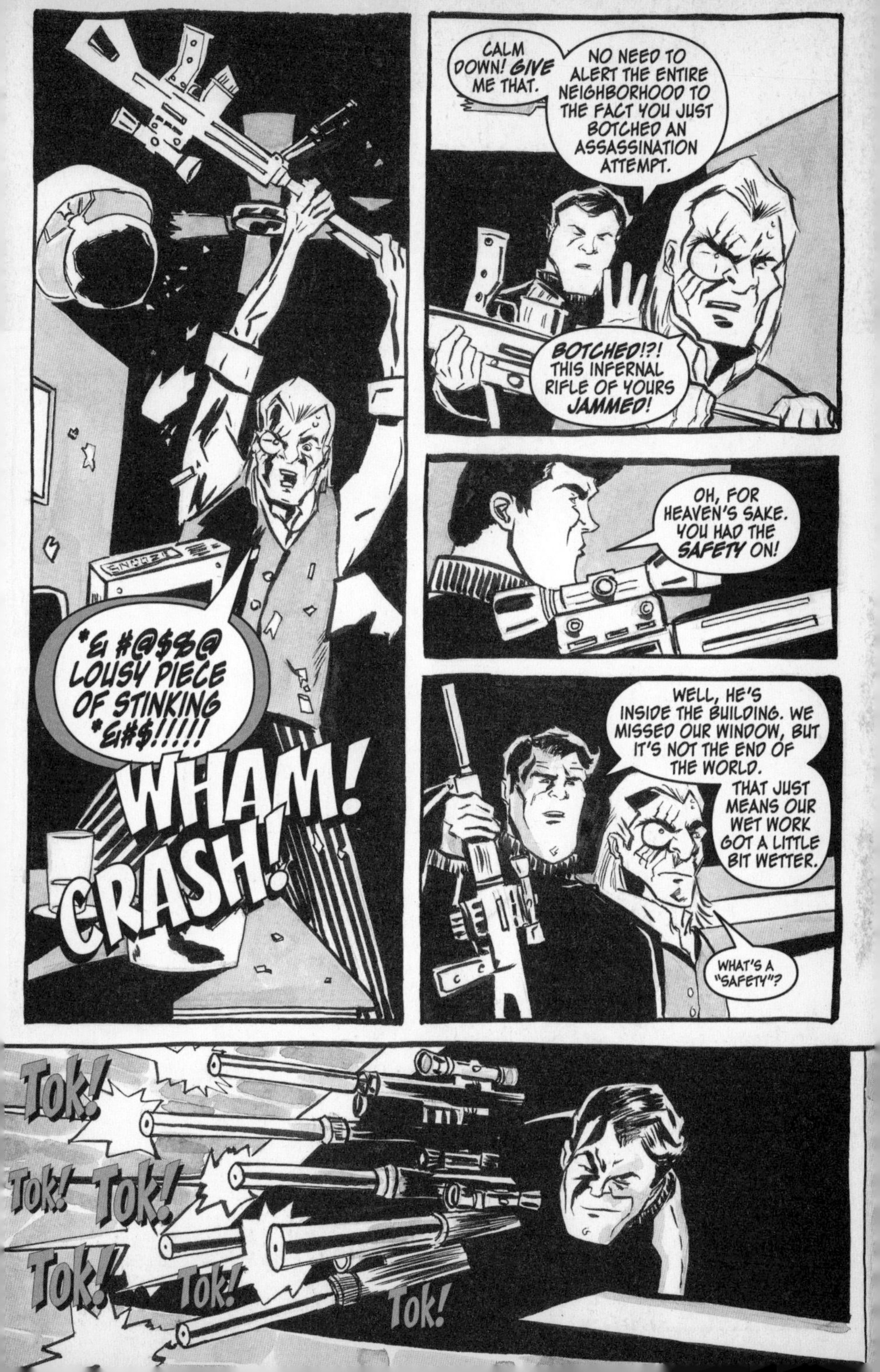
*&#@$$@ LOUSY PIECE OF STINKING *&#$!!!!!
WHAM!
CRASH!
CALM DOWN! GIVE ME THAT.
NO NEED TO ALERT THE ENTIRE NEIGHBORHOOD TO THE FACT YOU JUST BOTCHED AN ASSASSINATION ATTEMPT.
BOTCHED!?! THIS INFERNAL RIFLE OF YOURS JAMMED!
OH, FOR HEAVEN'S SAKE. YOU HAD THE SAFETY ON!
WELL, HE'S INSIDE THE BUILDING. WE MISSED OUR WINDOW, BUT IT'S NOT THE END OF THE WORLD.
THAT JUST MEANS OUR WET WORK GOT A LITTLE BIT WETTER.
WHAT'S A "SAFETY"?
TOK!
TOK! TOK!
TOK!
TOK!
TOK!

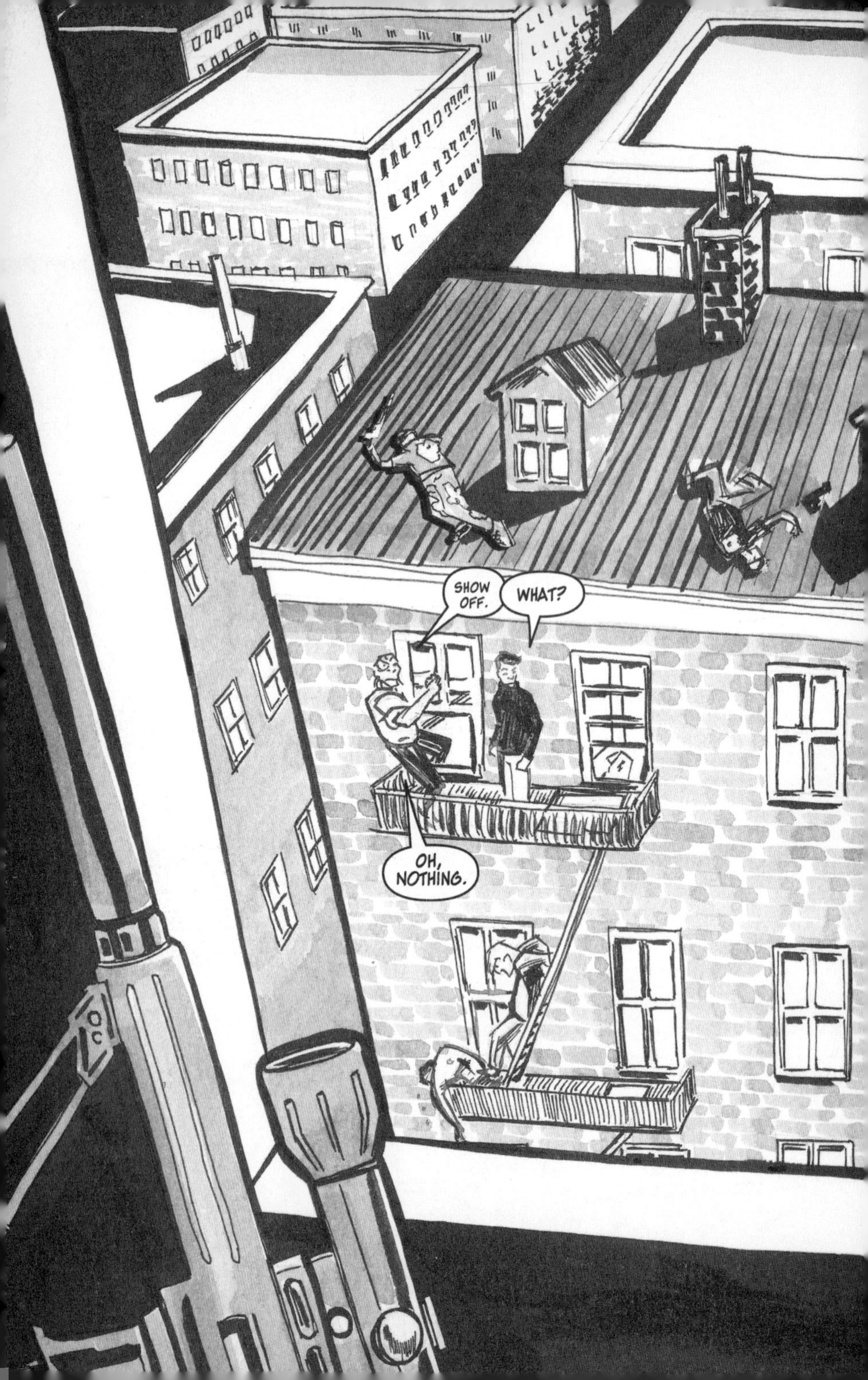
SHOW OFF.
WHAT?
OH, NOTHING.

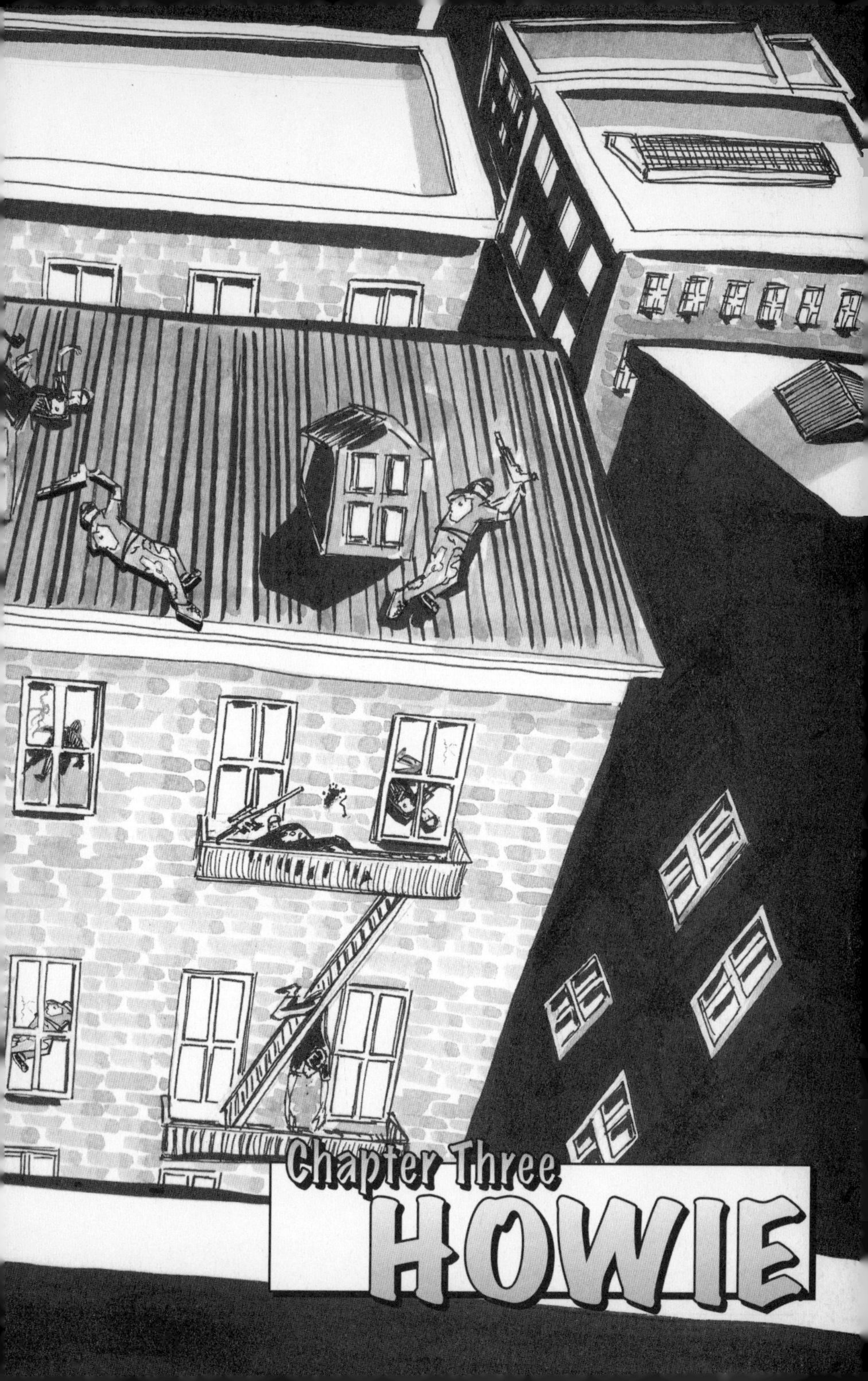
Chapter Three
HOWIE

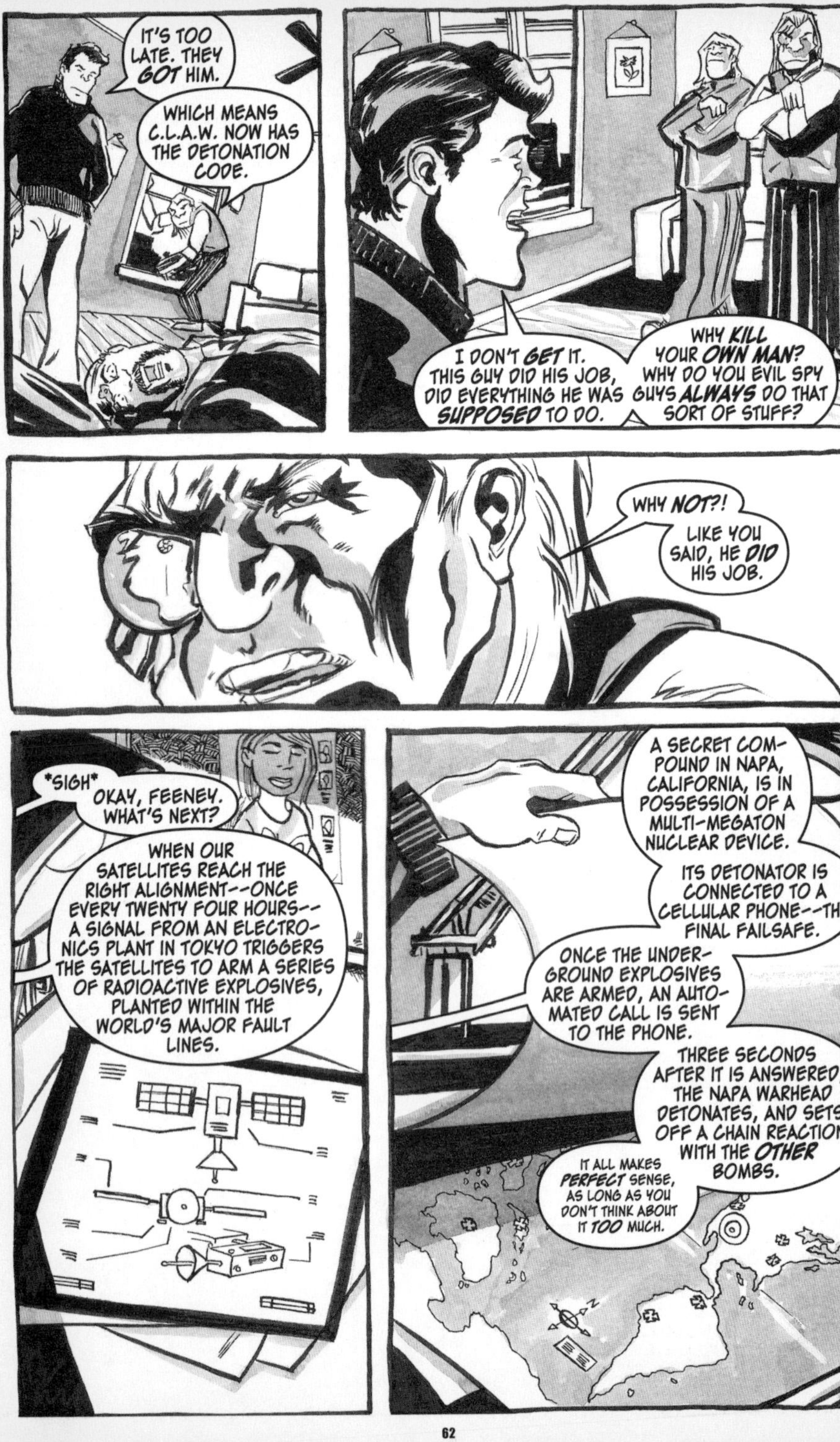
IT'S TOO LATE. THEY GOT HIM.
WHICH MEANS C.L.A.W. NOW HAS THE DETONATION CODE.
I DON'T GET IT. THIS GUY DID HIS JOB, DID EVERYTHING HE WAS SUPPOSED TO DO.
WHY KILL YOUR OWN MAN? WHY DO YOU EVIL SPY GUYS ALWAYS DO THAT SORT OF STUFF?
WHY NOT?!
LIKE YOU SAID, HE DID HIS JOB.
*SIGH* OKAY, FEENEY. WHAT'S NEXT?
WHEN OUR SATELLITES REACH THE RIGHT ALIGNMENT--ONCE EVERY TWENTY FOUR HOURS--A SIGNAL FROM AN ELECTRONICS PLANT IN TOKYO TRIGGERS THE SATELLITES TO ARM A SERIES OF RADIOACTIVE EXPLOSIVES, PLANTED WITHIN THE WORLD'S MAJOR FAULT LINES.
A SECRET COMPOUND IN NAPA, CALIFORNIA, IS IN POSSESSION OF A MULTI-MEGATON NUCLEAR DEVICE.
ITS DETONATOR IS CONNECTED TO A CELLULAR PHONE--THE FINAL FAILSAFE.
ONCE THE UNDERGROUND EXPLOSIVES ARE ARMED, AN AUTOMATED CALL IS SENT TO THE PHONE.
THREE SECONDS AFTER IT IS ANSWERED, THE NAPA WARHEAD DETONATES, AND SETS OFF A CHAIN REACTION WITH THE OTHER BOMBS.
IT ALL MAKES PERFECT SENSE, AS LONG AS YOU DON'T THINK ABOUT IT TOO MUCH.

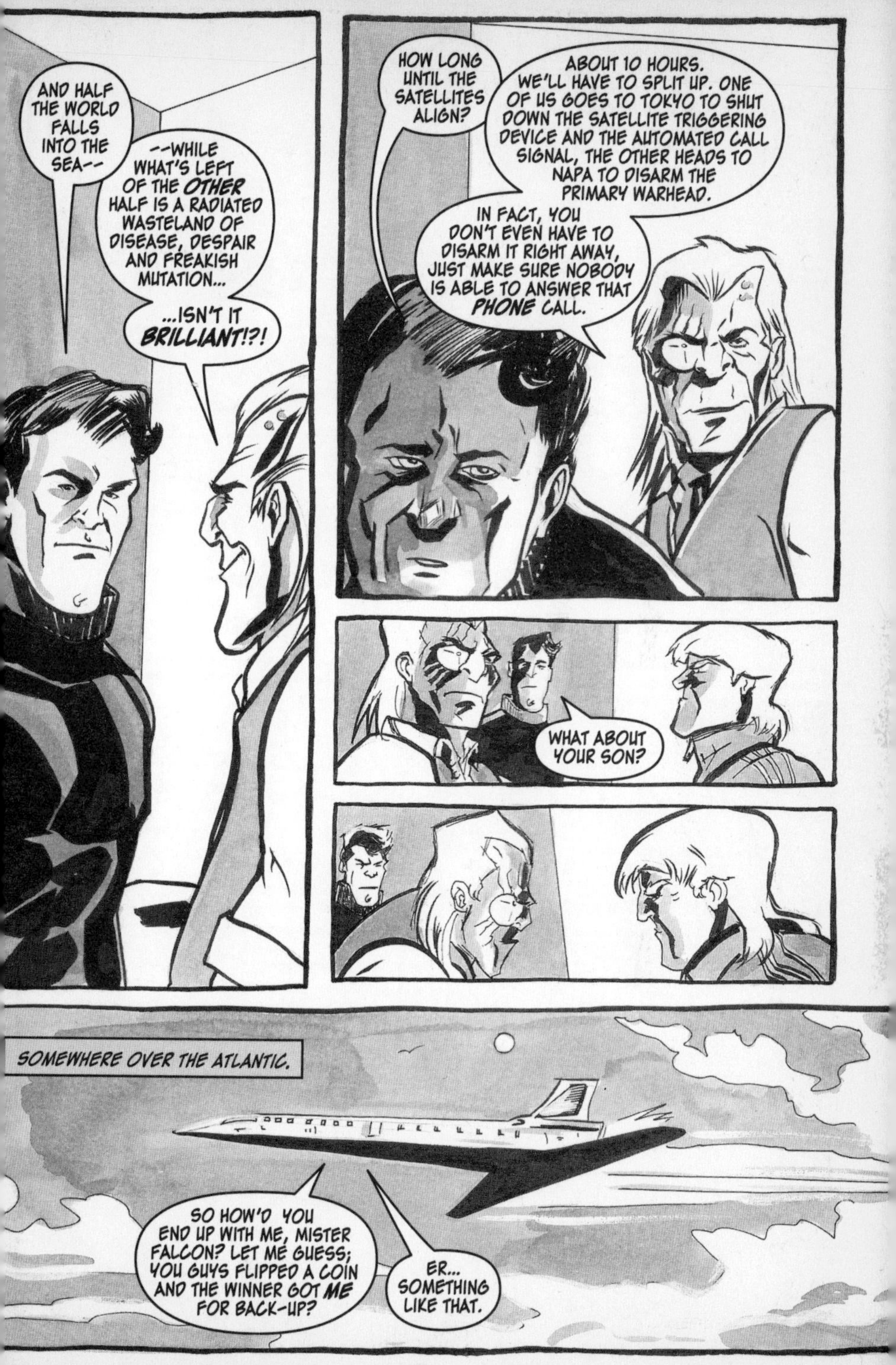
AND HALF THE WORLD FALLS INTO THE SEA--
--WHILE WHAT'S LEFT OF THE *OTHER* HALF IS A RADIATED WASTELAND OF DISEASE, DESPAIR AND FREAKISH MUTATION...
...ISN'T IT *BRILLIANT*!?!
HOW LONG UNTIL THE SATELLITES ALIGN?
ABOUT 10 HOURS. WE'LL HAVE TO SPLIT UP. ONE OF US GOES TO TOKYO TO SHUT DOWN THE SATELLITE TRIGGERING DEVICE AND THE AUTOMATED CALL SIGNAL, THE OTHER HEADS TO NAPA TO DISARM THE PRIMARY WARHEAD.
IN FACT, YOU DON'T EVEN HAVE TO DISARM IT RIGHT AWAY, JUST MAKE SURE NOBODY IS ABLE TO ANSWER THAT *PHONE* CALL.
WHAT ABOUT YOUR SON?
SOMEWHERE OVER THE ATLANTIC.
SO HOW'D YOU END UP WITH ME, MISTER FALCON? LET ME GUESS; YOU GUYS FLIPPED A COIN AND THE WINNER GOT *ME* FOR BACK-UP?
ER... SOMETHING LIKE THAT.

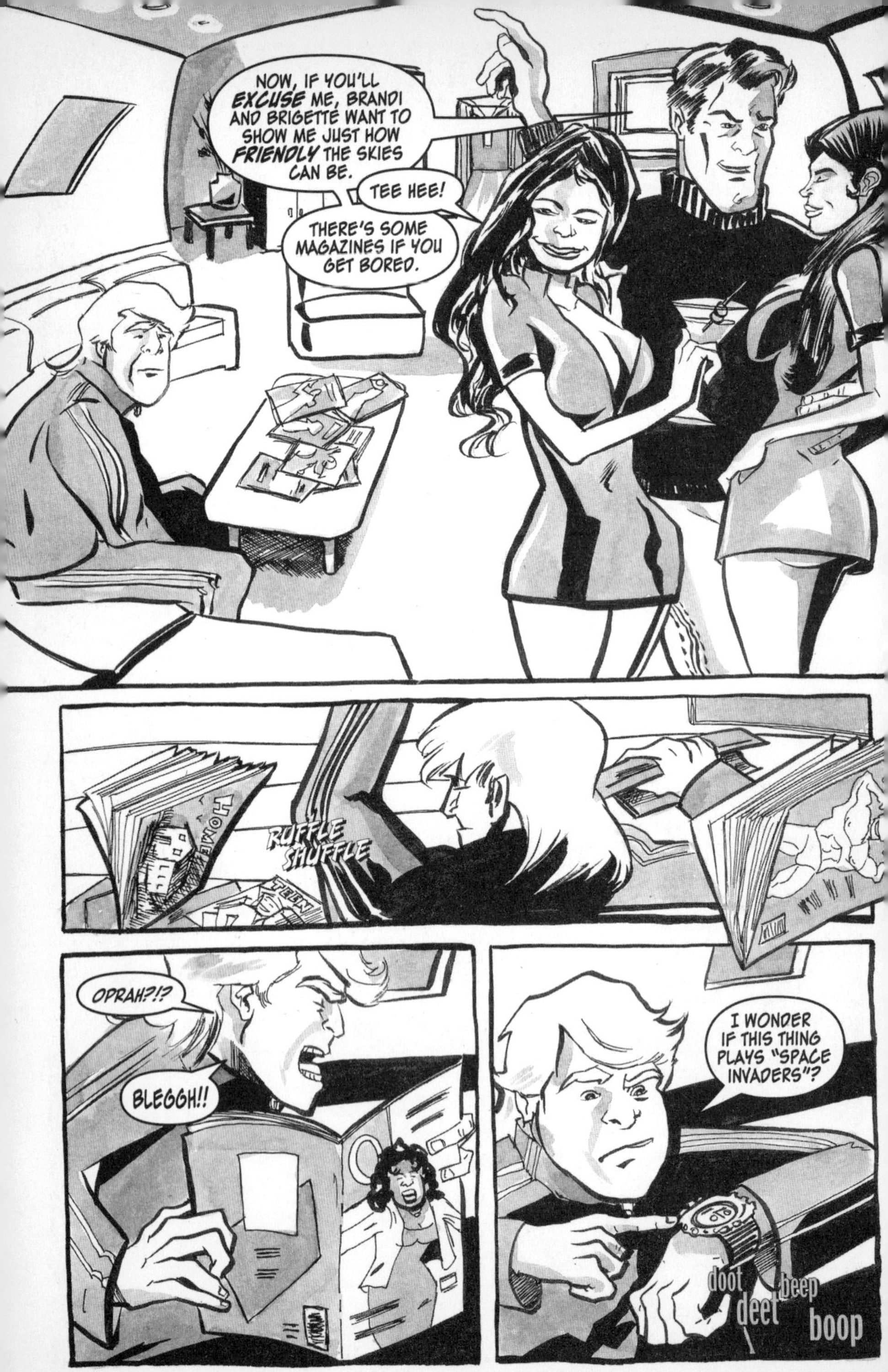

NOW, IF YOU'LL EXCUSE ME, BRANDI AND BRIGETTE WANT TO SHOW ME JUST HOW FRIENDLY THE SKIES CAN BE.
TEE HEE!
THERE'S SOME MAGAZINES IF YOU GET BORED.
RUFFLE SHUFFLE
OPRAH?!?
BLEGGH!!
I WONDER IF THIS THING PLAYS "SPACE INVADERS"?
doot deet beep boop

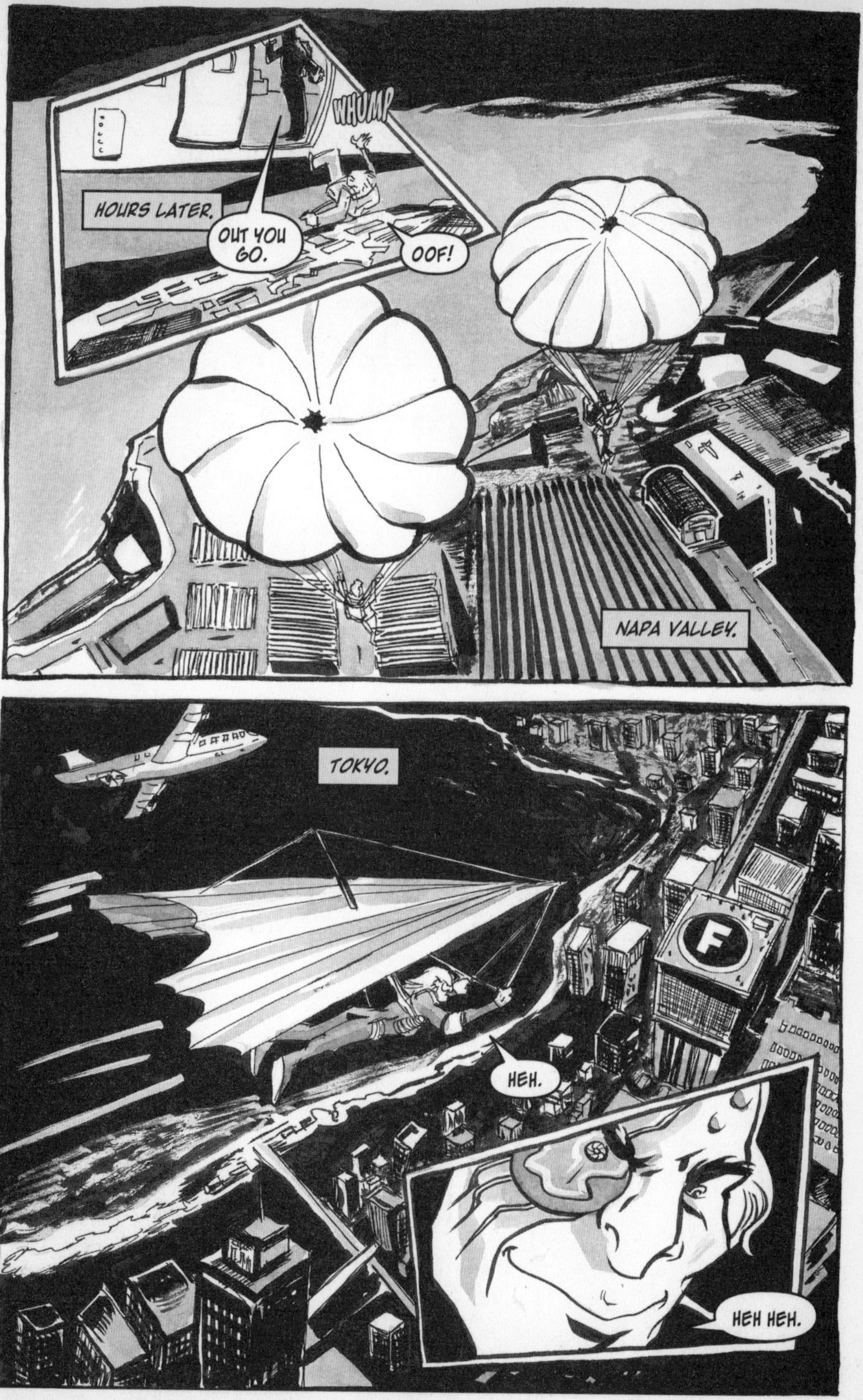
WHUMP
HOURS LATER.
OUT YOU GO.
OOF!
NAPA VALLEY.
TOKYO.
F
HEH.
HEH HEH.

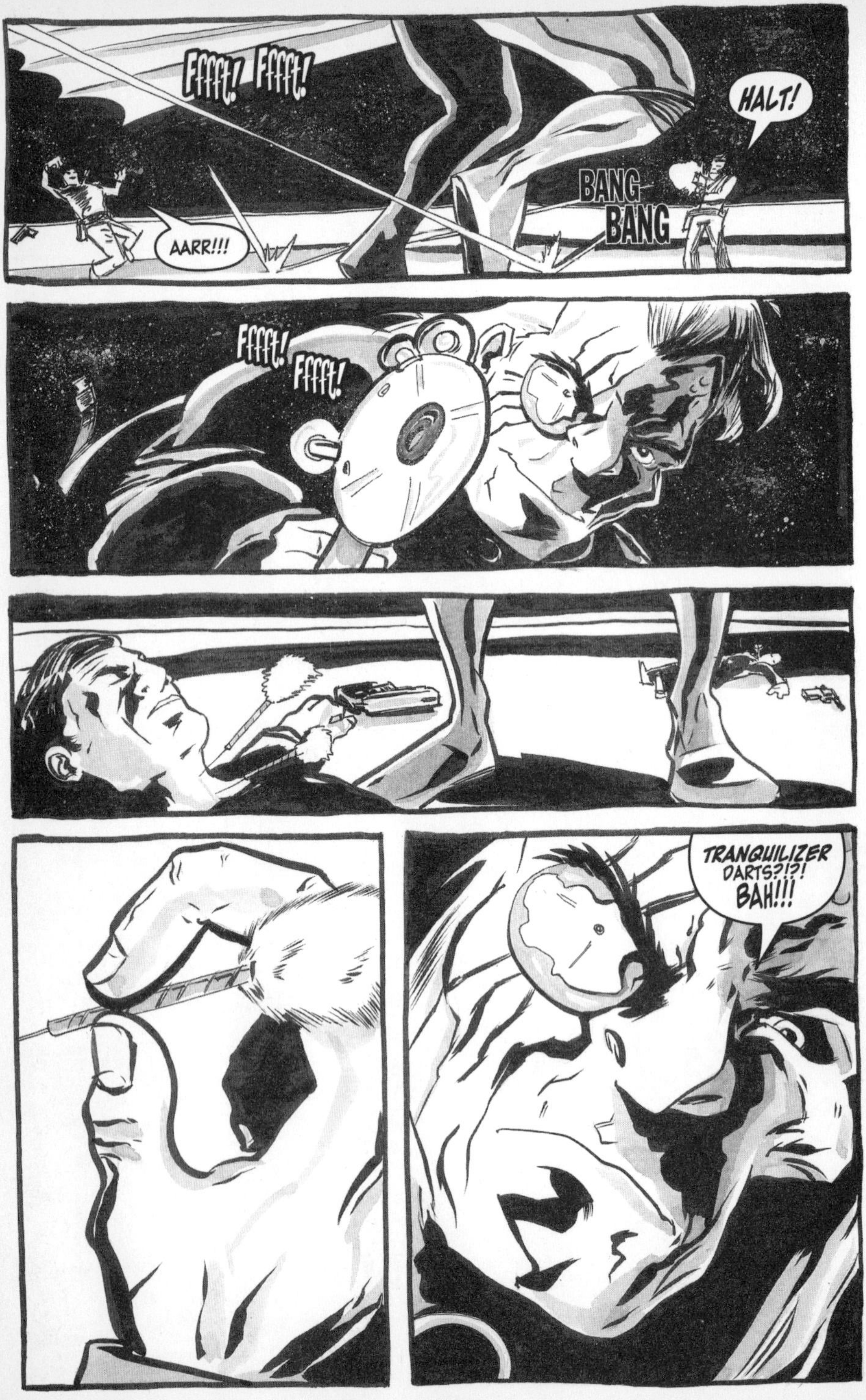
Fffft! Fffft!
HALT!
BANG
BANG
AARR!!!
Fffft!
Fffft!
TRANQUILIZER DARTS?!?! BAH!!!

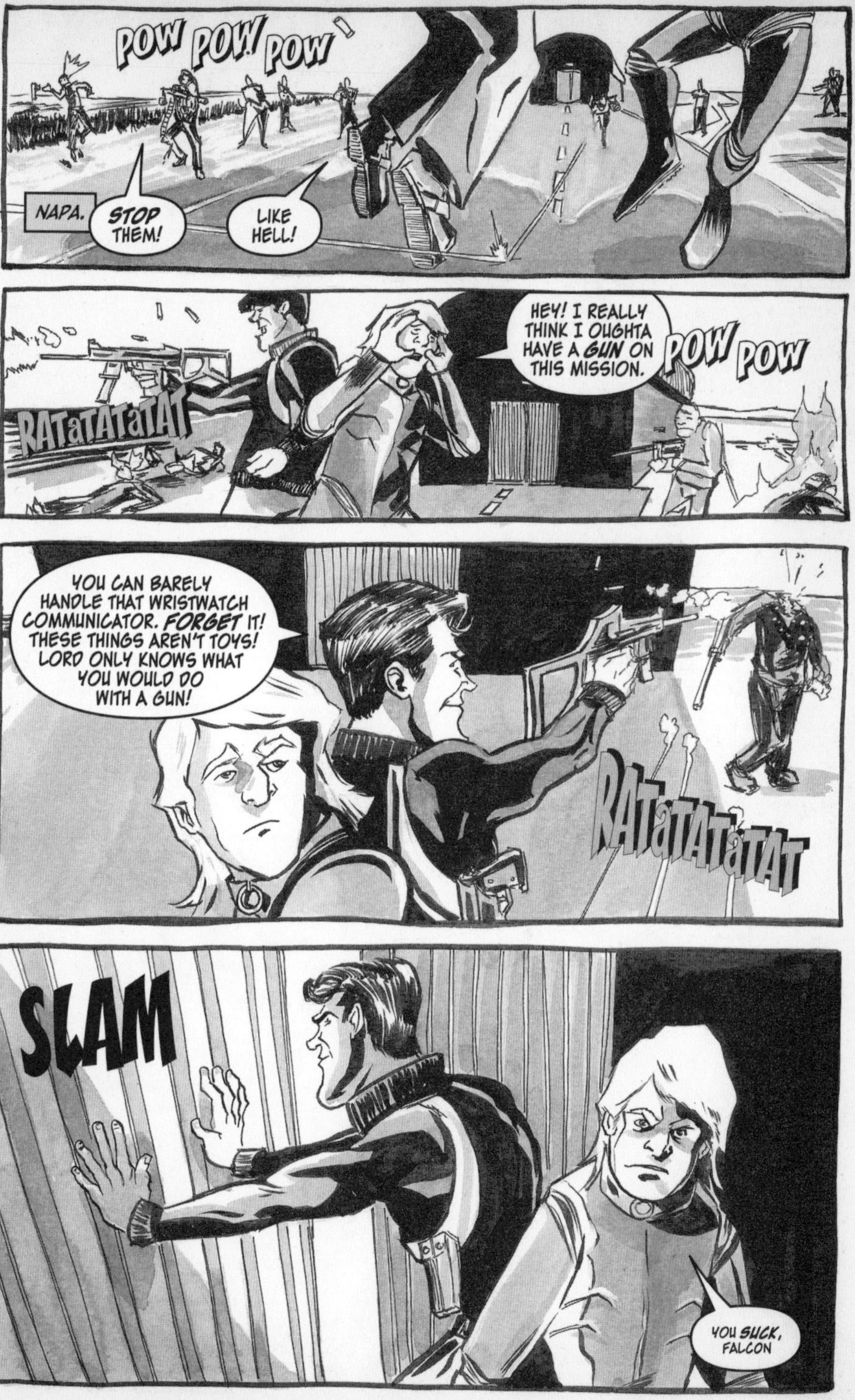
POW POW! POW
NAPA.
STOP THEM!
LIKE HELL!
RATATATATAT
HEY! I REALLY THINK I OUGHTA HAVE A GUN ON THIS MISSION.
POW POW
YOU CAN BARELY HANDLE THAT WRISTWATCH COMMUNICATOR. FORGET IT! THESE THINGS AREN'T TOYS! LORD ONLY KNOWS WHAT YOU WOULD DO WITH A GUN!
RATATATATATAT
SLAM
YOU SUCK, FALCON

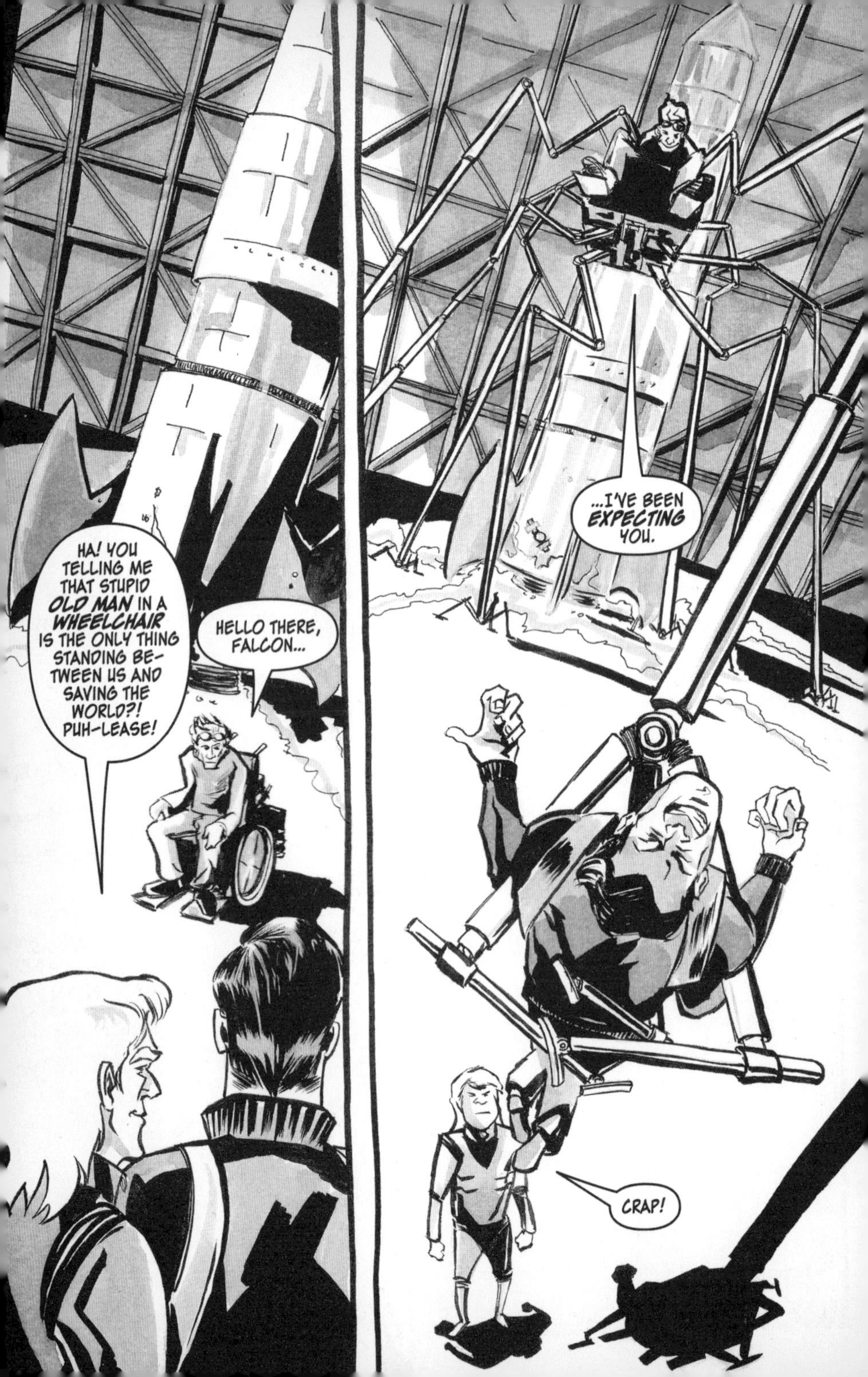
HA! YOU TELLING ME THAT STUPID OLD MAN IN A WHEELCHAIR IS THE ONLY THING STANDING BE-TWEEN US AND SAVING THE WORLD?! PUH-LEASE!
HELLO THERE, FALCON...
...I'VE BEEN EXPECTING YOU.
CRAP!

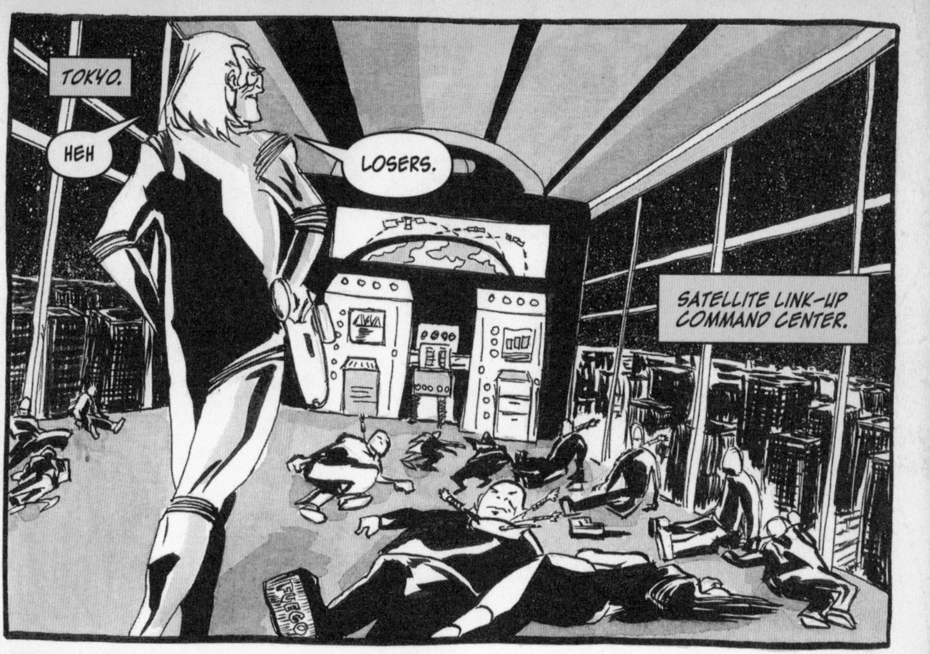
TOKYO.
HEH
LOSERS.
SATELLITE LINK-UP COMMAND CENTER.
FUEGO

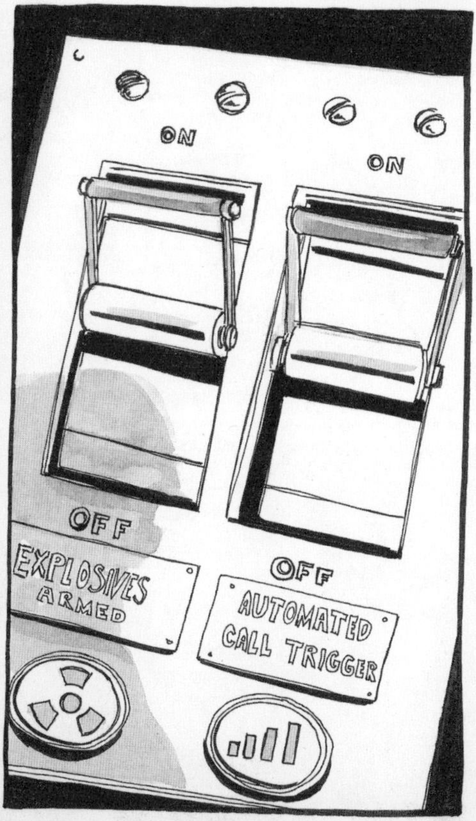
ON
ON
OFF
EXPLOSIVES ARMED
OFF
AUTOMATED CALL TRIGGER

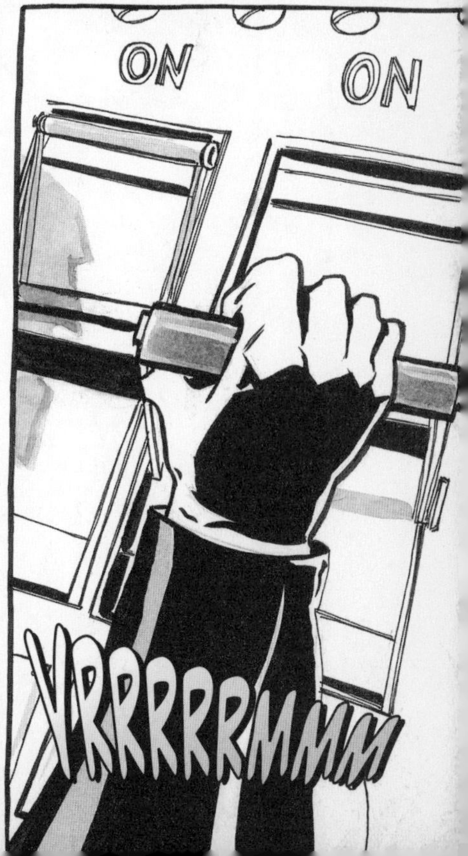
ON
ON
VRRRRRMMMM

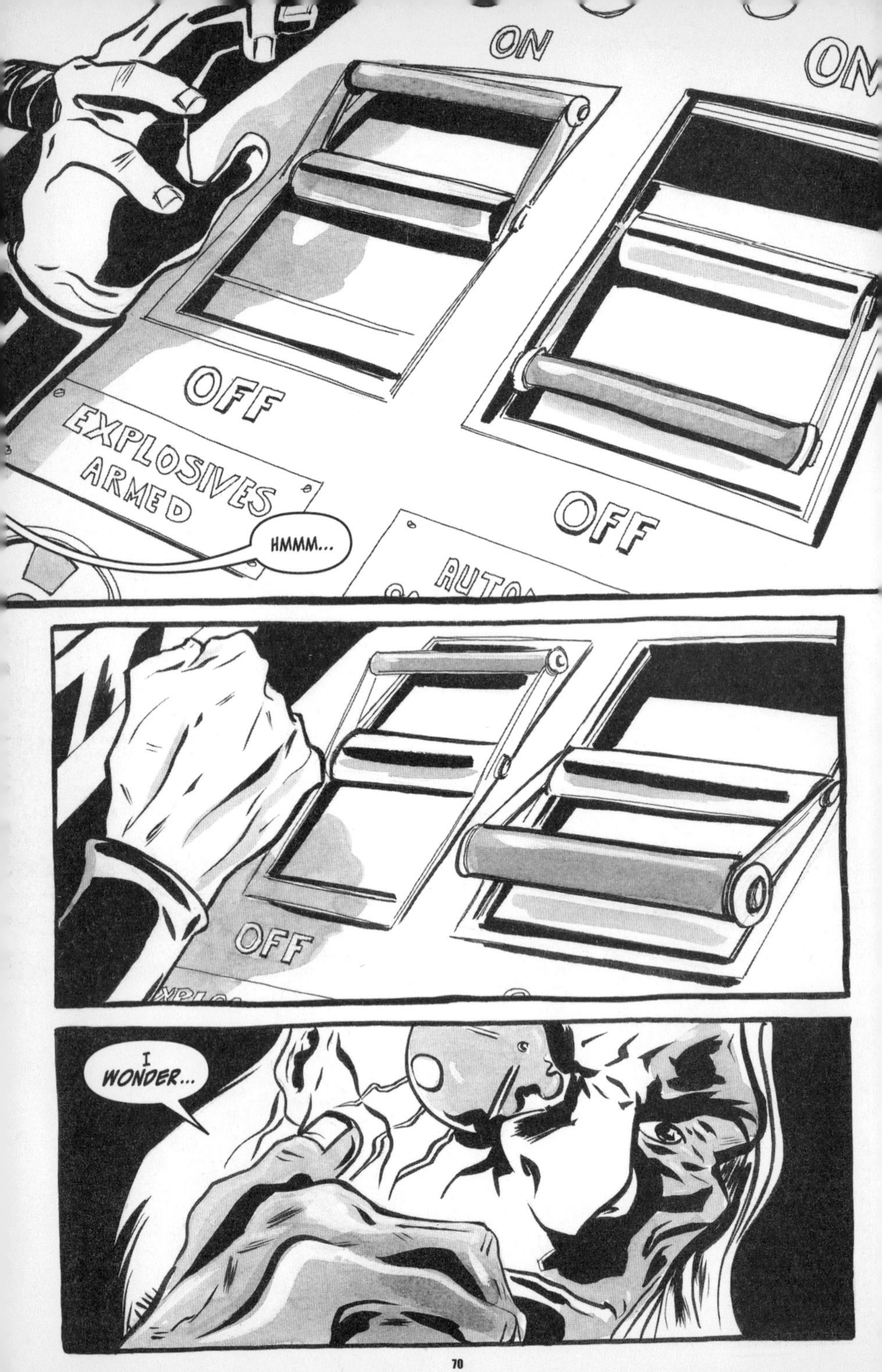
ON
ON
OFF
EXPLOSIVES ARMED
OFF
HMMM...
OFF
I WONDER...

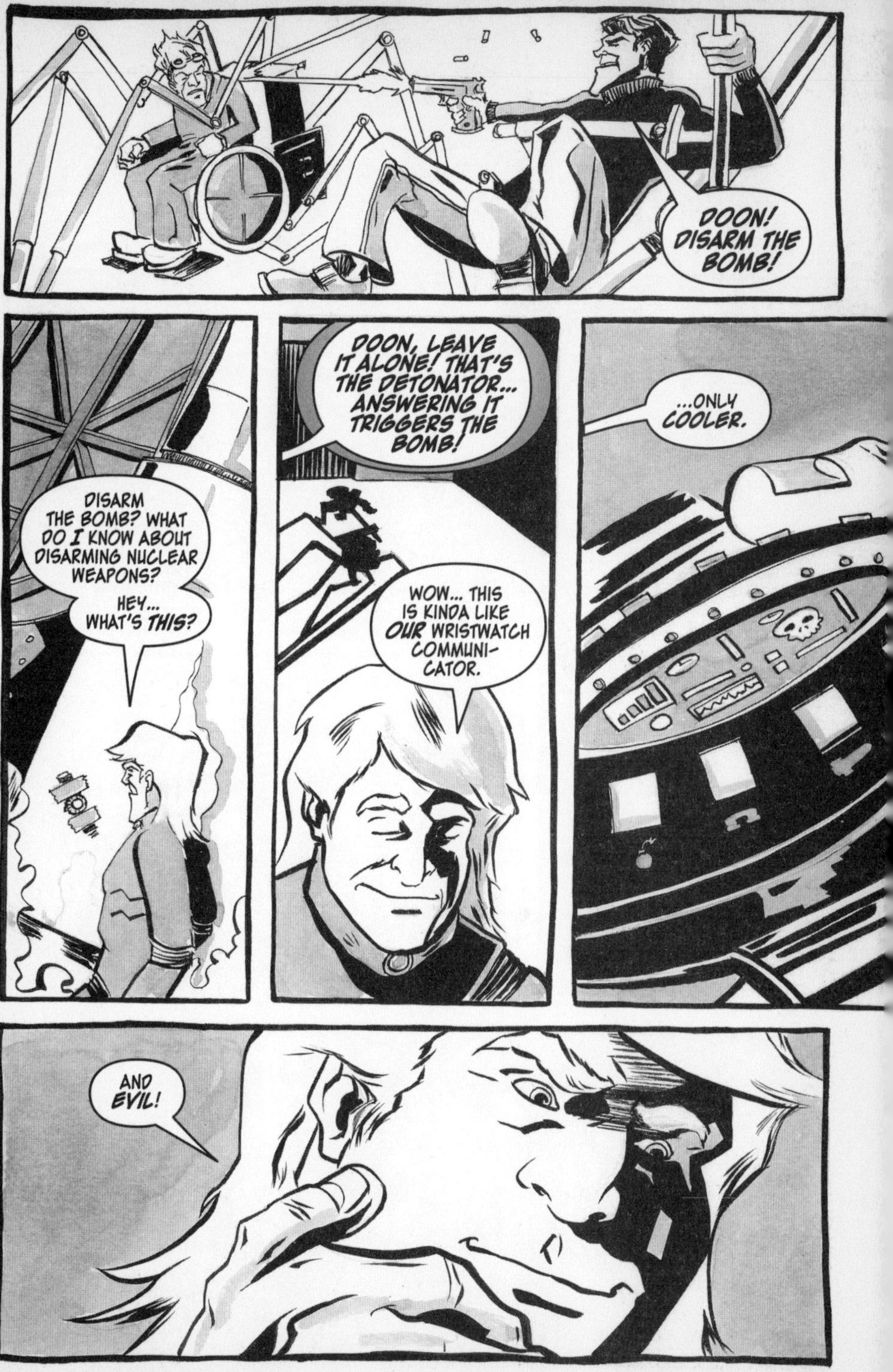
DOON! DISARM THE BOMB!
DISARM THE BOMB? WHAT DO I KNOW ABOUT DISARMING NUCLEAR WEAPONS?
HEY... WHAT'S THIS?
DOON, LEAVE IT ALONE! THAT'S THE DETONATOR... ANSWERING IT TRIGGERS THE BOMB!
WOW... THIS IS KINDA LIKE OUR WRISTWATCH COMMUNI-CATOR.
...ONLY COOLER.
AND EVIL!

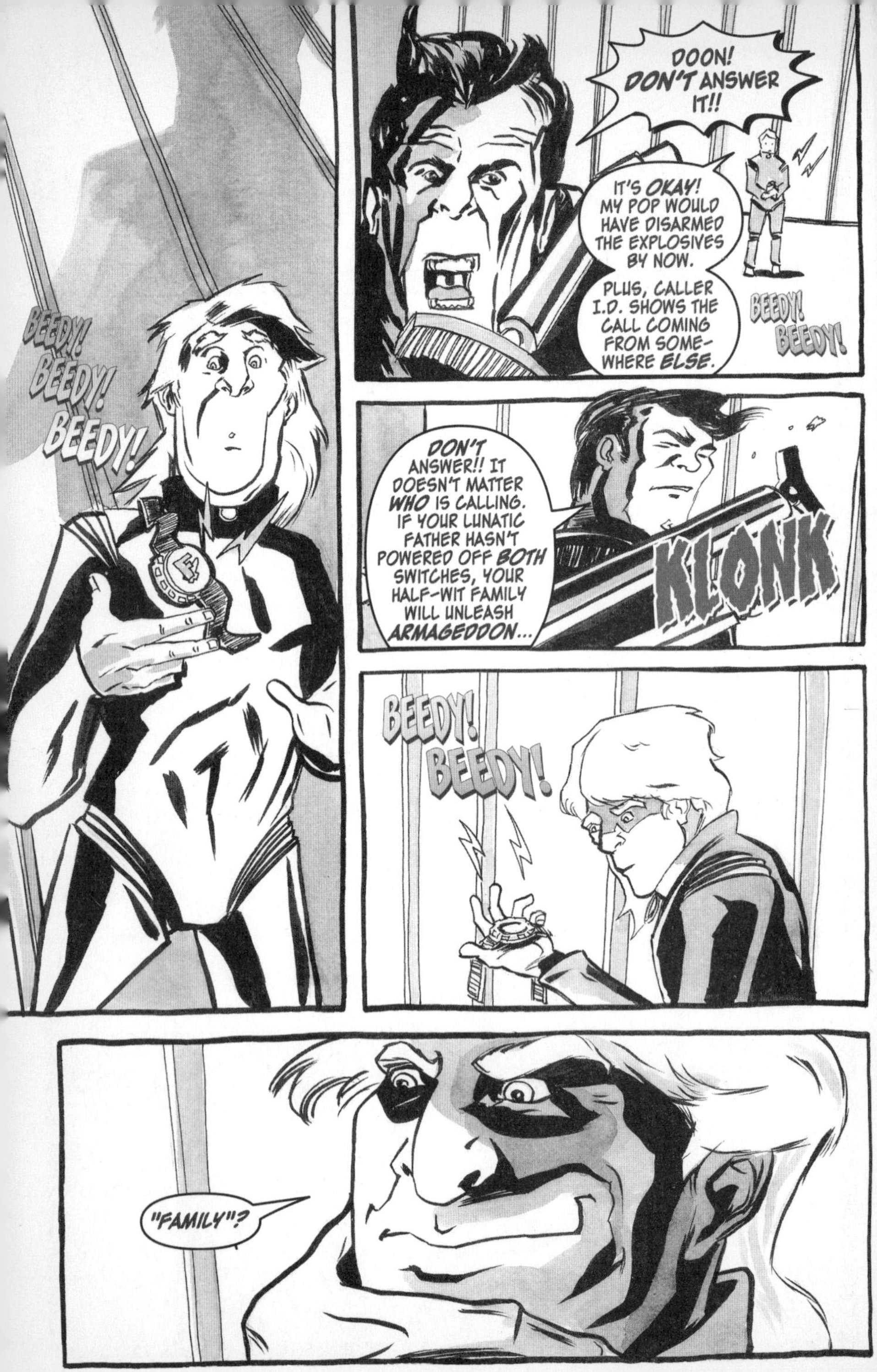
BEEDY! BEEDY! BEEDY!
DOON! DON'T ANSWER IT!!
IT'S OKAY! MY POP WOULD HAVE DISARMED THE EXPLOSIVES BY NOW.
PLUS, CALLER I.D. SHOWS THE CALL COMING FROM SOME-WHERE ELSE.
BEEDY! BEEDY!
DON'T ANSWER!! IT DOESN'T MATTER WHO IS CALLING. IF YOUR LUNATIC FATHER HASN'T POWERED OFF BOTH SWITCHES, YOUR HALF-WIT FAMILY WILL UNLEASH ARMAGEDDON...
KLONK
BEEDY! BEEDY!
"FAMILY"?

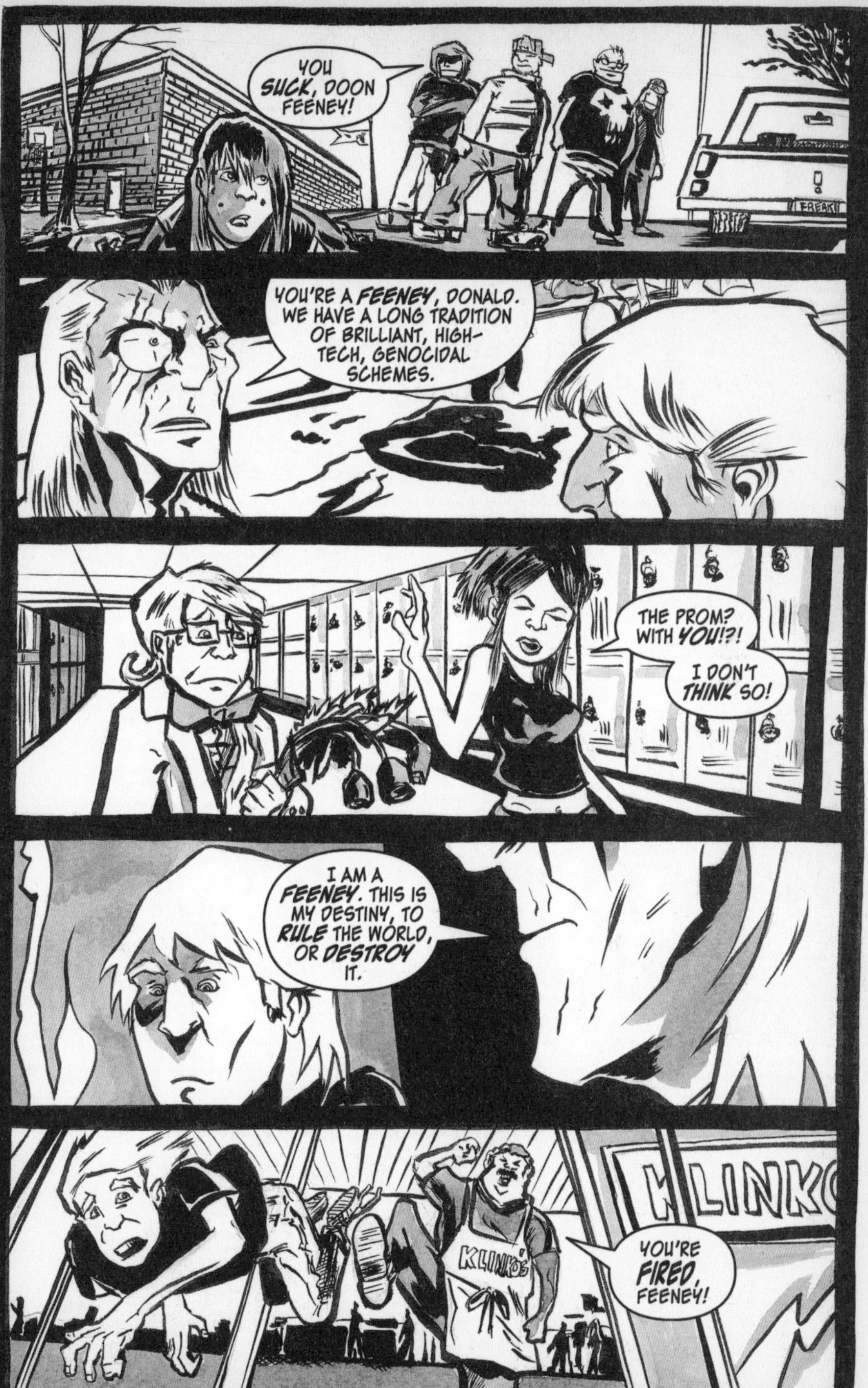

YOU SUCK, DOON FEENEY!
FREAK
YOU'RE A FEENEY, DONALD. WE HAVE A LONG TRADITION OF BRILLIANT, HIGH-TECH, GENOCIDAL SCHEMES.
THE PROM? WITH YOU!?!
I DON'T THINK SO!
I AM A FEENEY. THIS IS MY DESTINY, TO RULE THE WORLD, OR DESTROY IT.
KLINKO'S
YOU'RE FIRED, FEENEY!

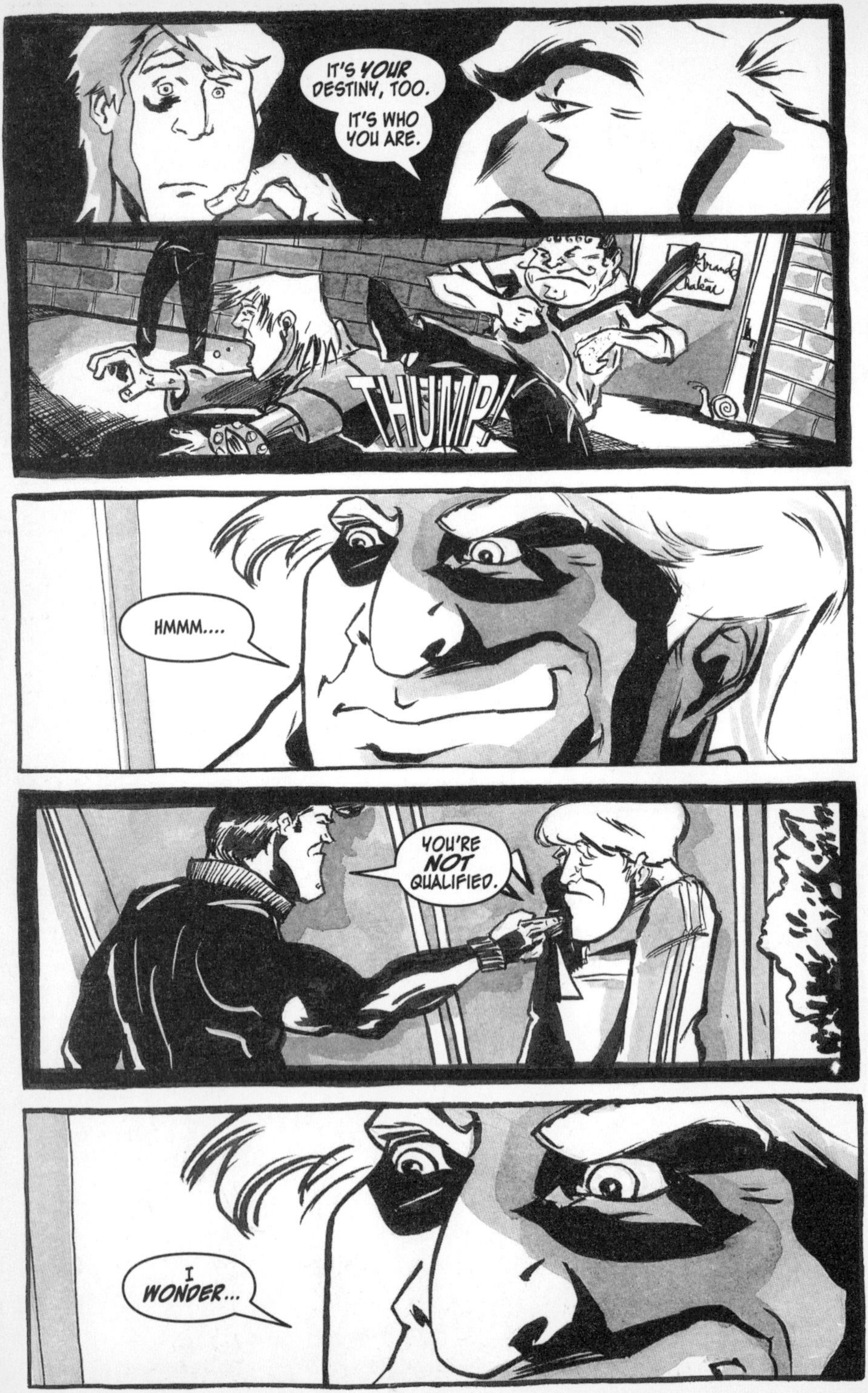
IT'S YOUR DESTINY, TOO.
IT'S WHO YOU ARE.
THUMP!
HMMM....
YOU'RE NOT QUALIFIED.
I WONDER...

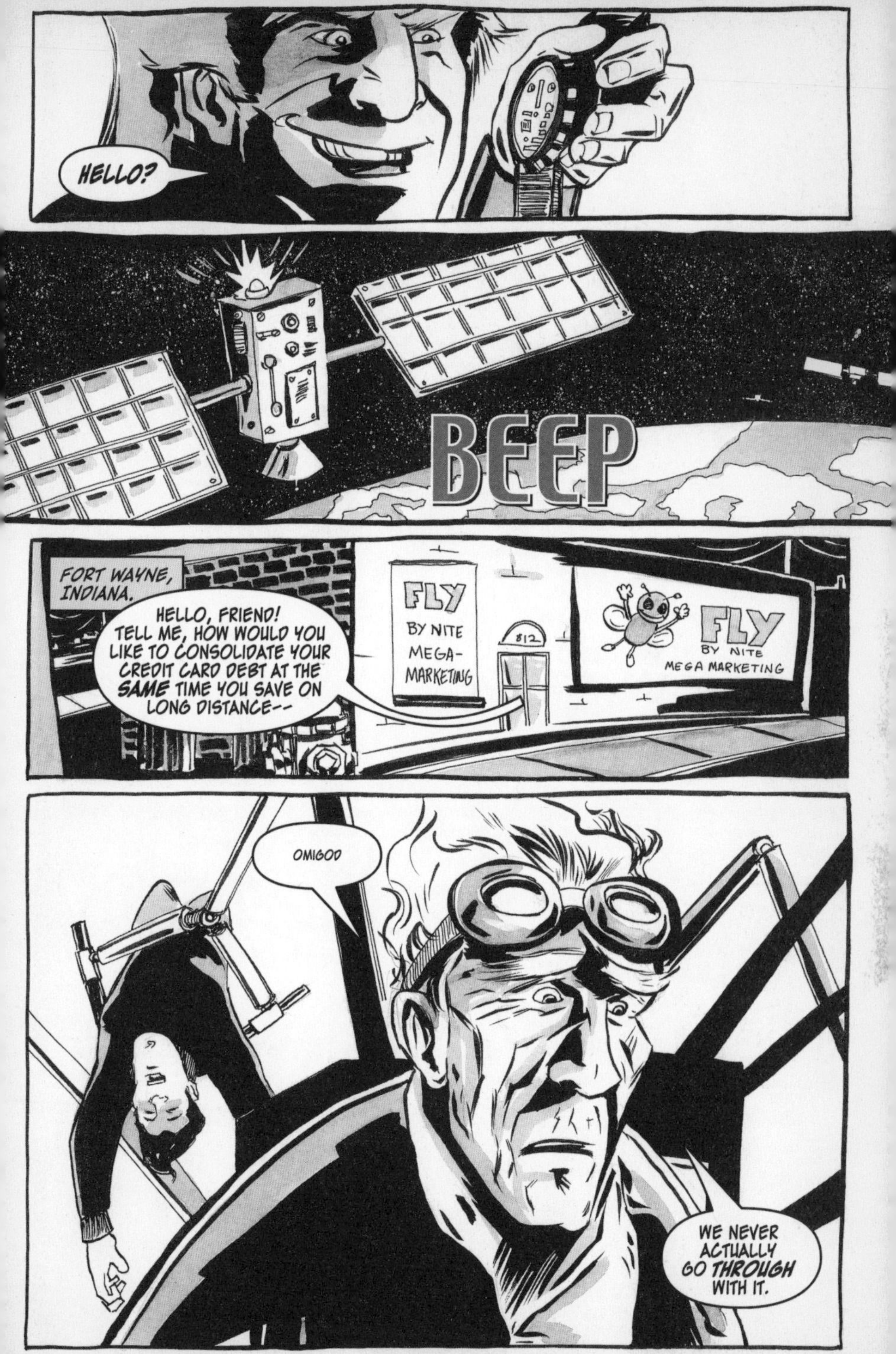
HELLO?
BEEP
FORT WAYNE, INDIANA.
HELLO, FRIEND! TELL ME, HOW WOULD YOU LIKE TO CONSOLIDATE YOUR CREDIT CARD DEBT AT THE SAME TIME YOU SAVE ON LONG DISTANCE--
FLY BY NITE MEGA-MARKETING
812
FLY BY NITE MEGA MARKETING
OMIGOD
WE NEVER ACTUALLY GO THROUGH WITH IT.

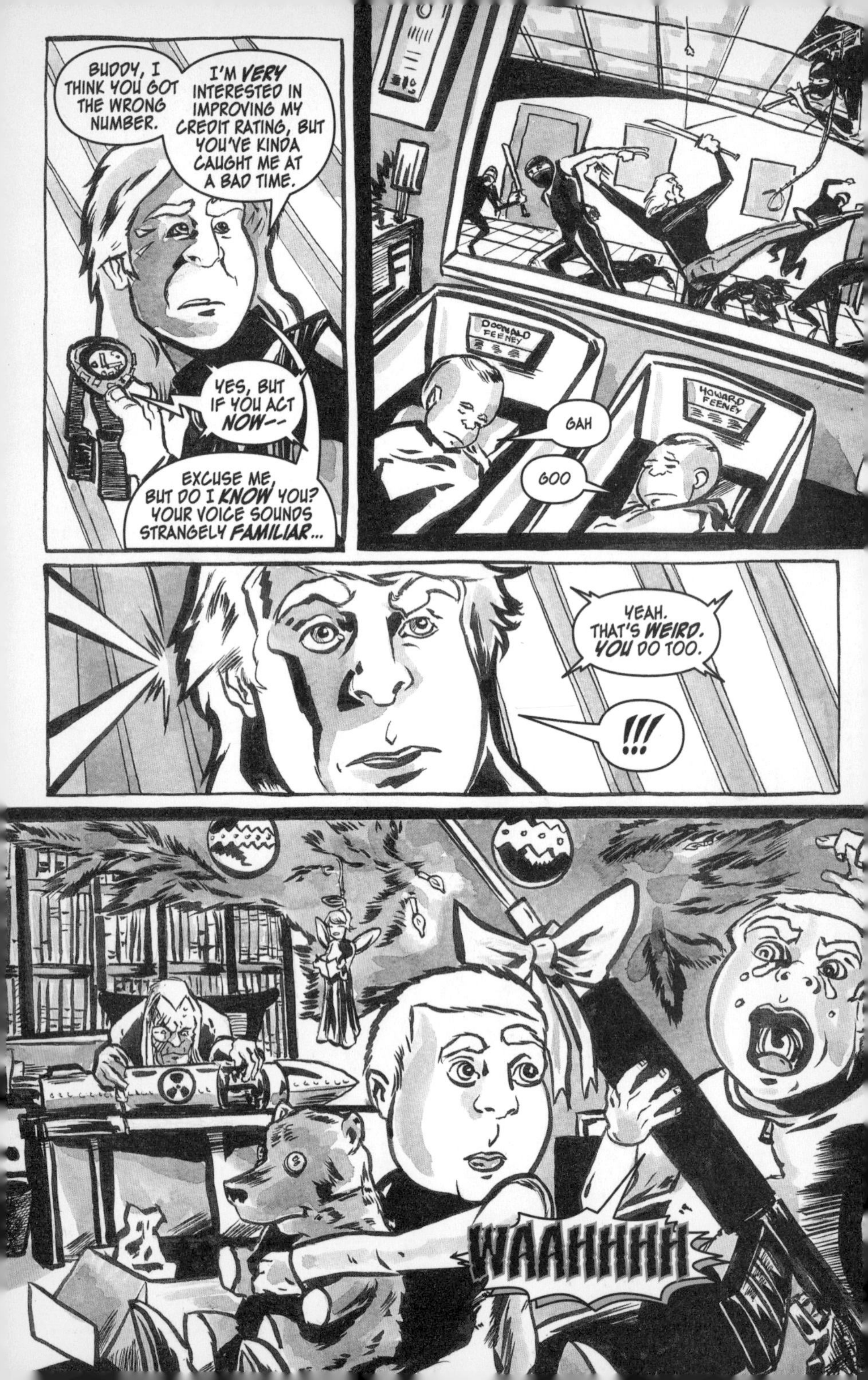

BUDDY, I THINK YOU GOT THE WRONG NUMBER.
I'M VERY INTERESTED IN IMPROVING MY CREDIT RATING, BUT YOU'VE KINDA CAUGHT ME AT A BAD TIME.
YES, BUT IF YOU ACT NOW--
EXCUSE ME, BUT DO I KNOW YOU? YOUR VOICE SOUNDS STRANGELY FAMILIAR...
DONALD FEENEY
HOWARD FEENEY
GAH
GOO
YEAH. THAT'S WEIRD. YOU DO TOO.
!!!
WAAHHHH

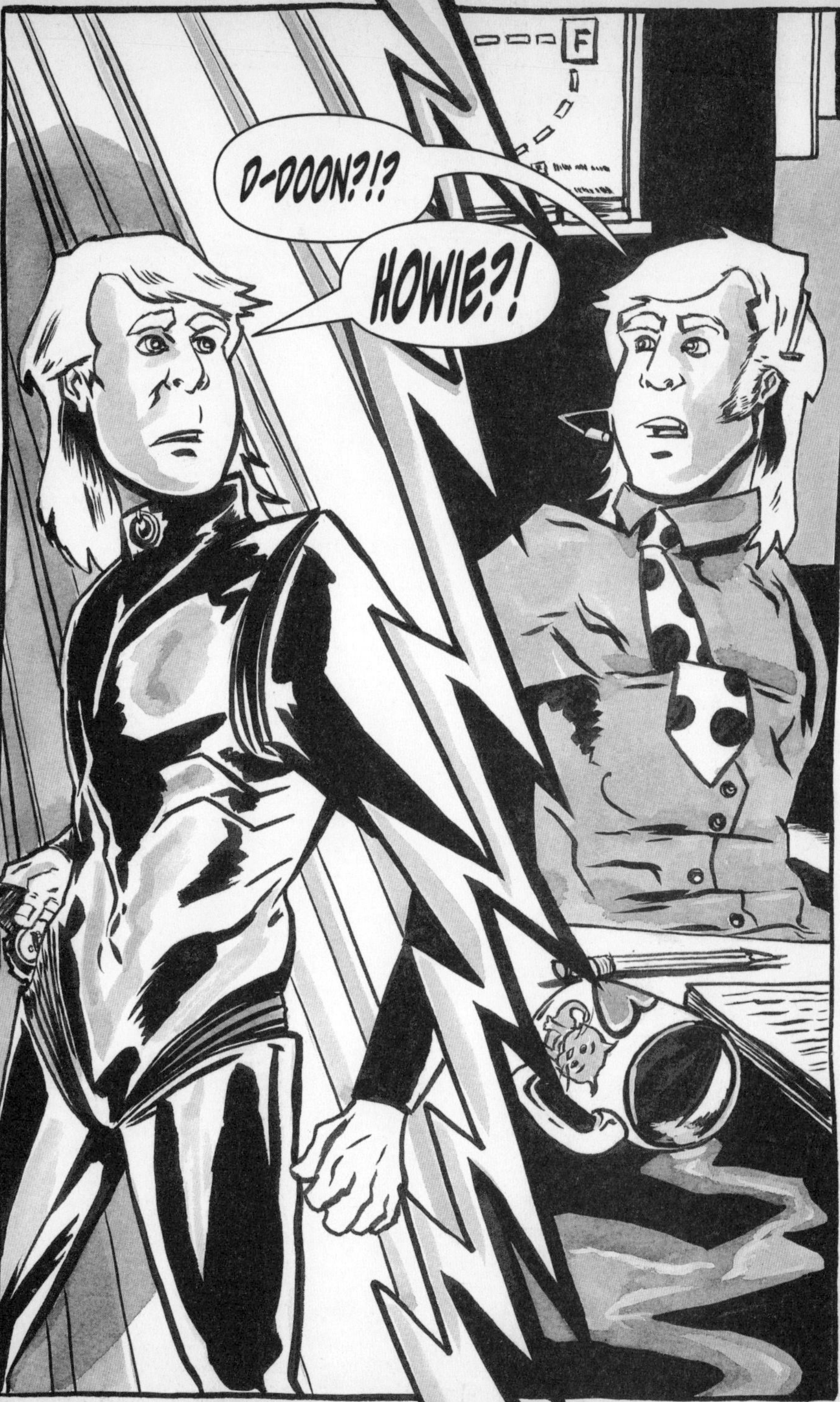
D-DOON?!?
HOWIE?!

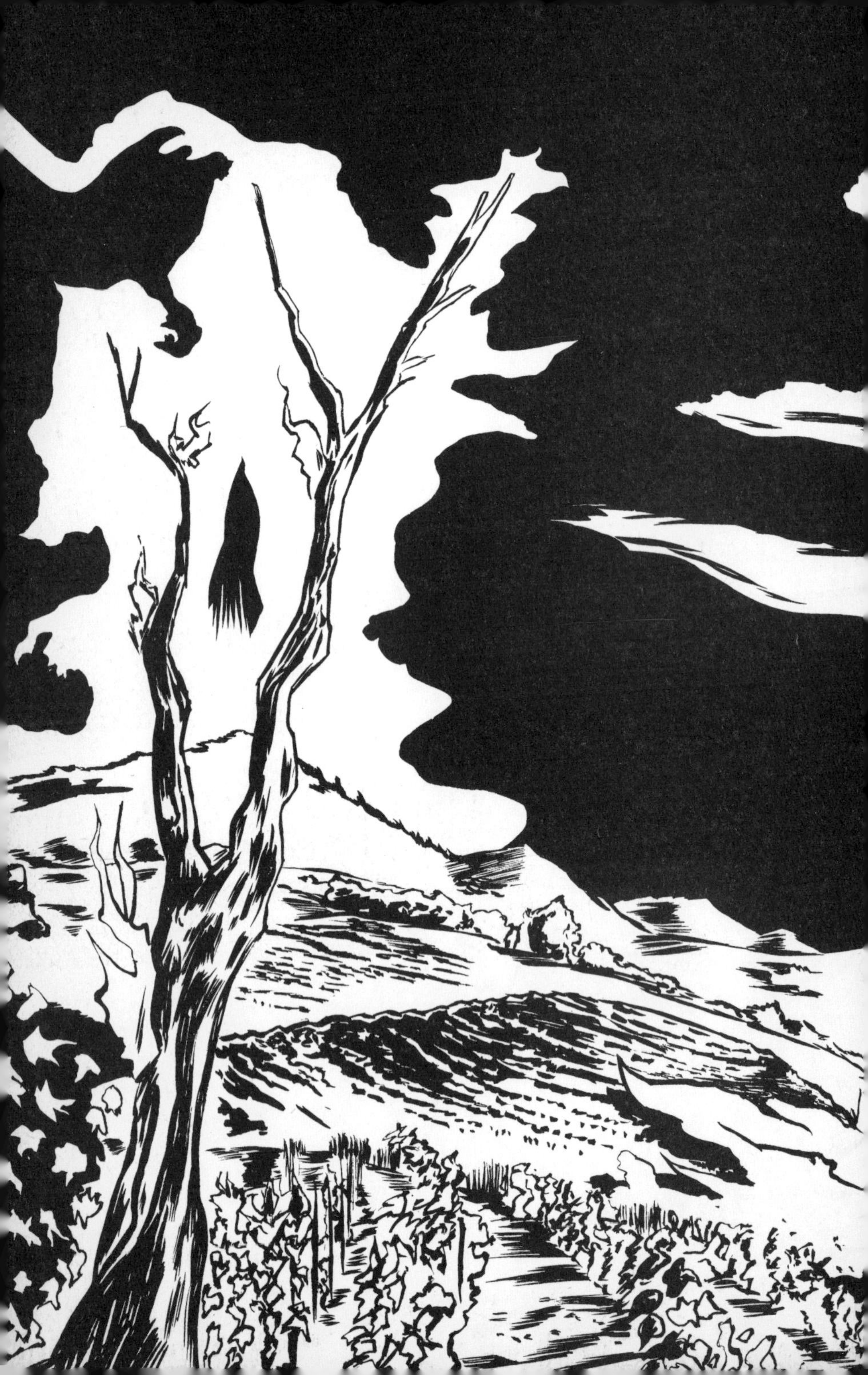

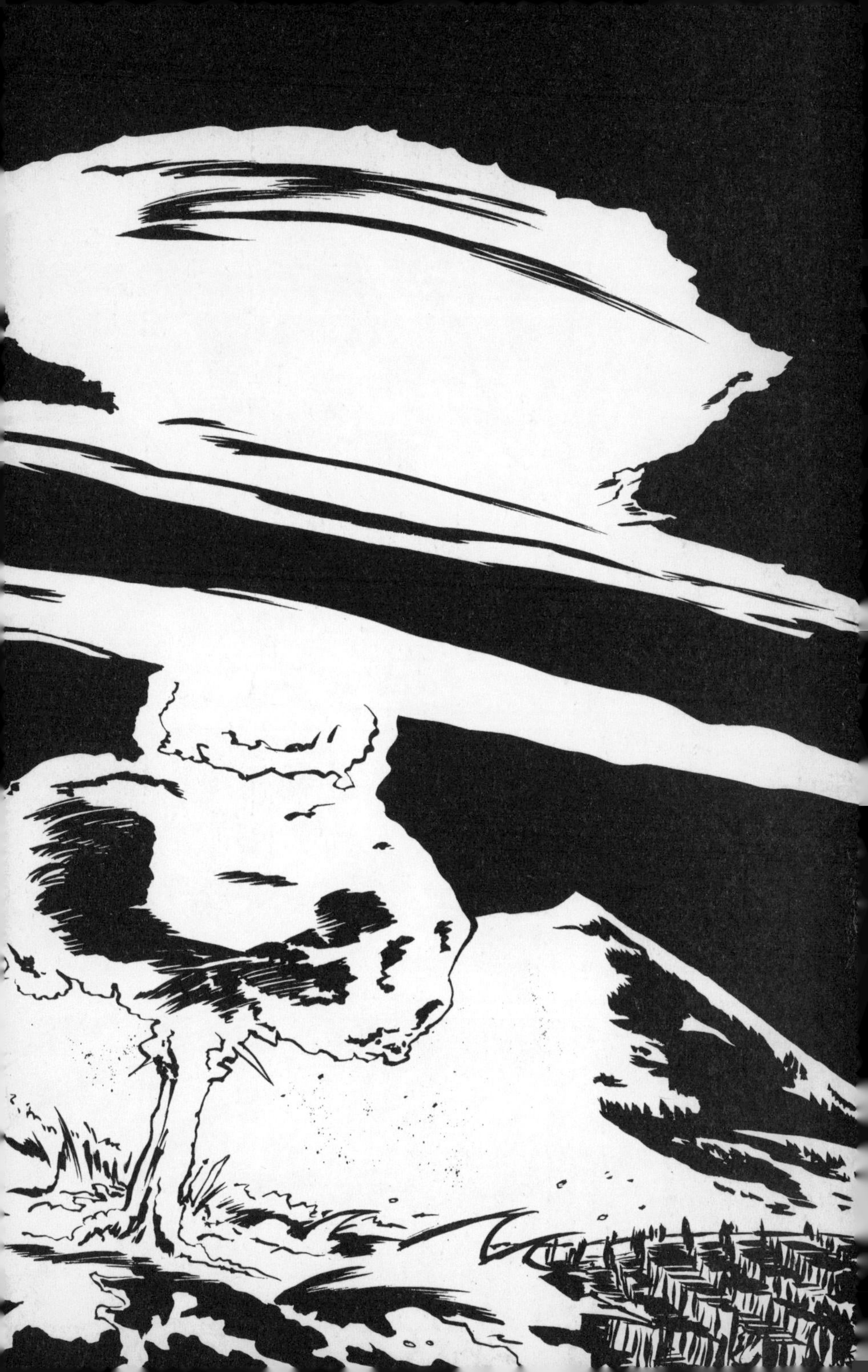

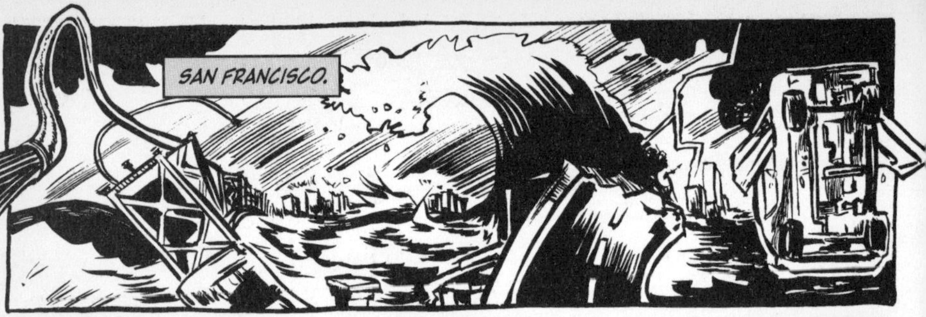
SAN FRANCISCO.

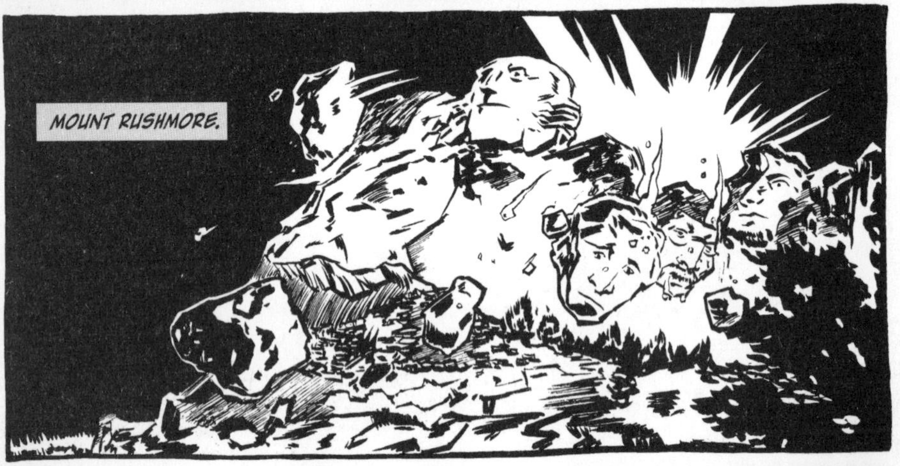
MOUNT RUSHMORE.

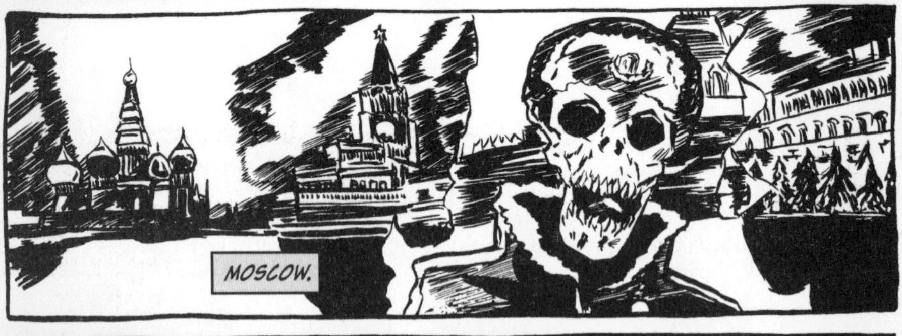
MOSCOW.

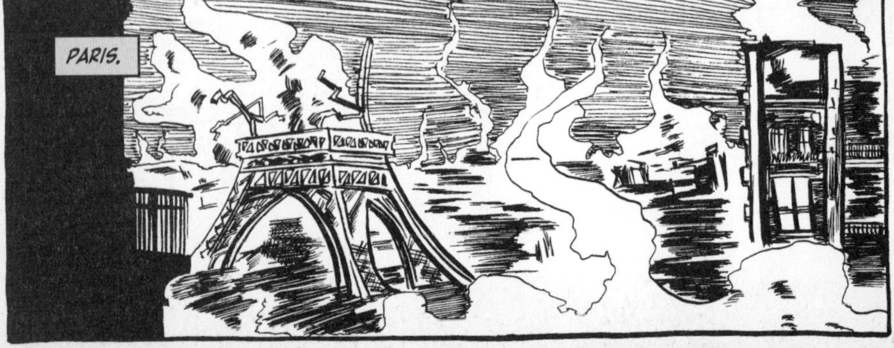
PARIS.

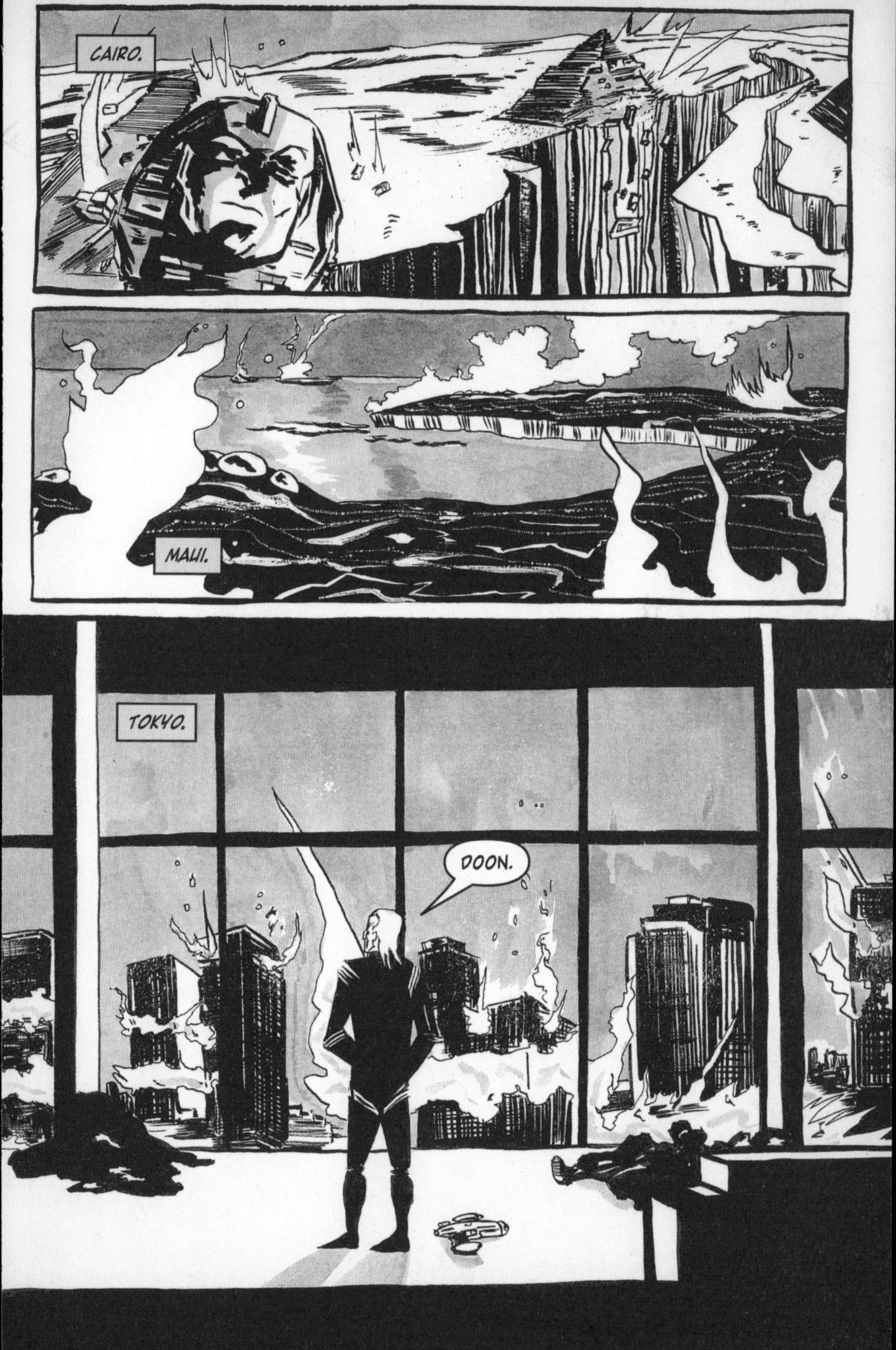
CAIRO.
MAUI.
TOKYO.
DOON.

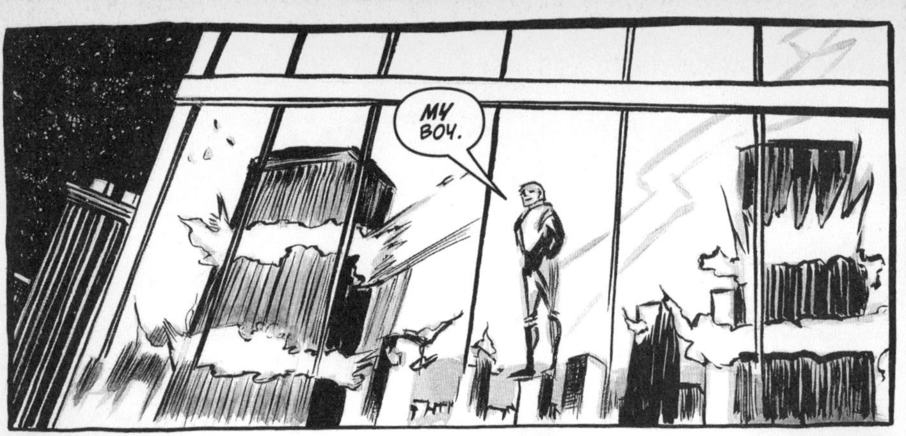
MY BOY.

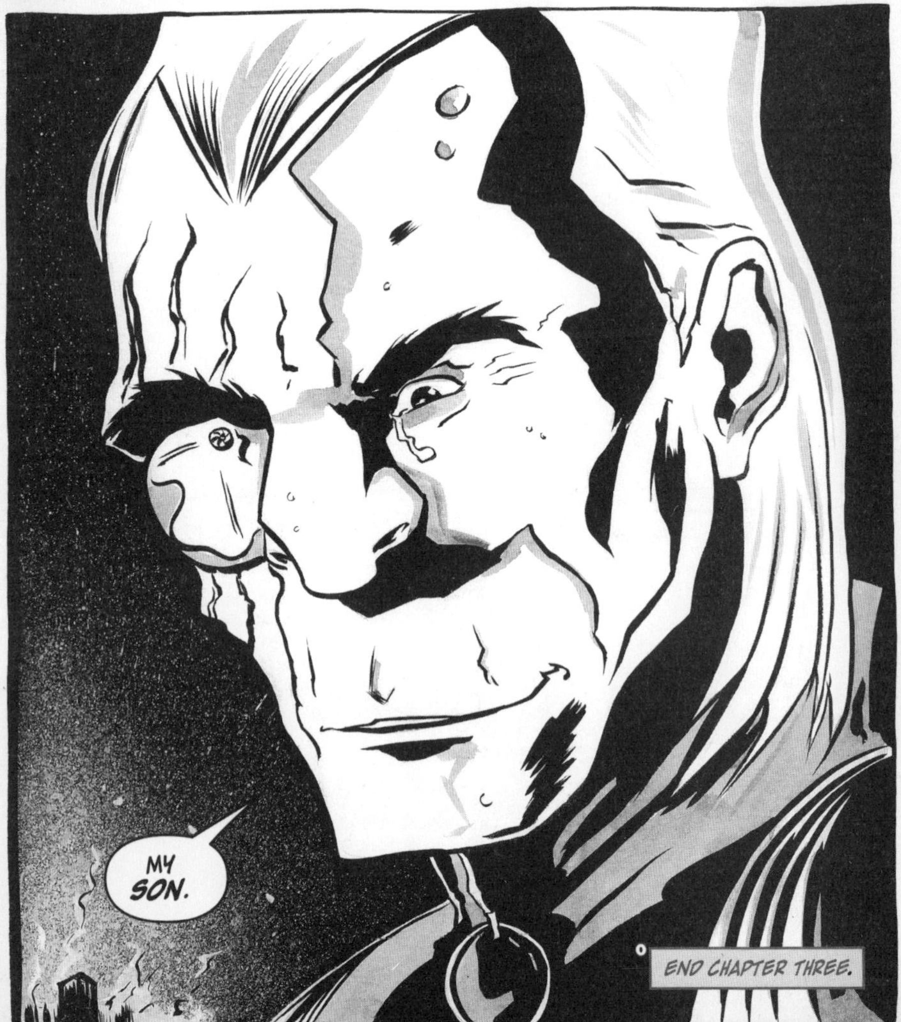
MY SON.
END CHAPTER THREE.

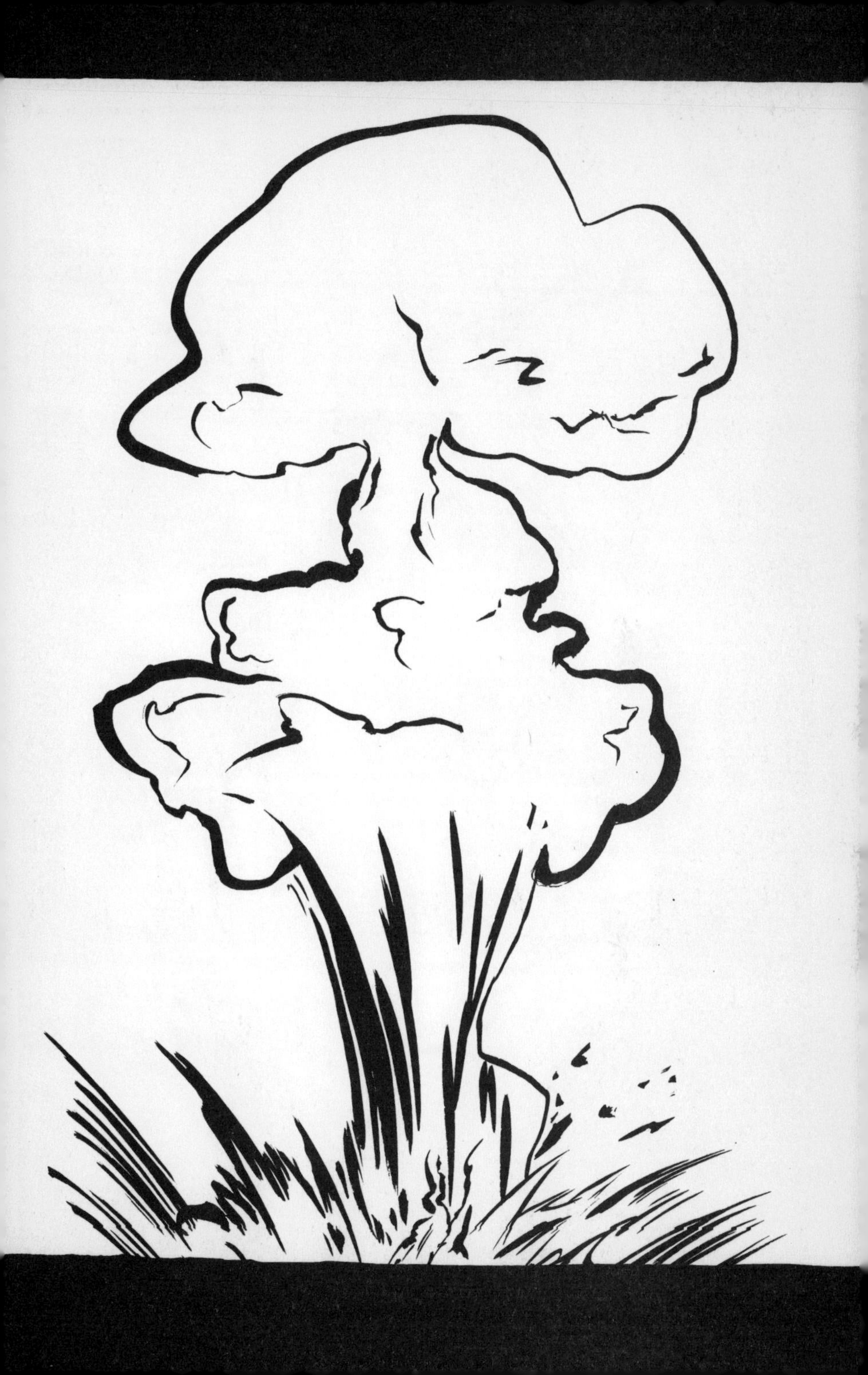

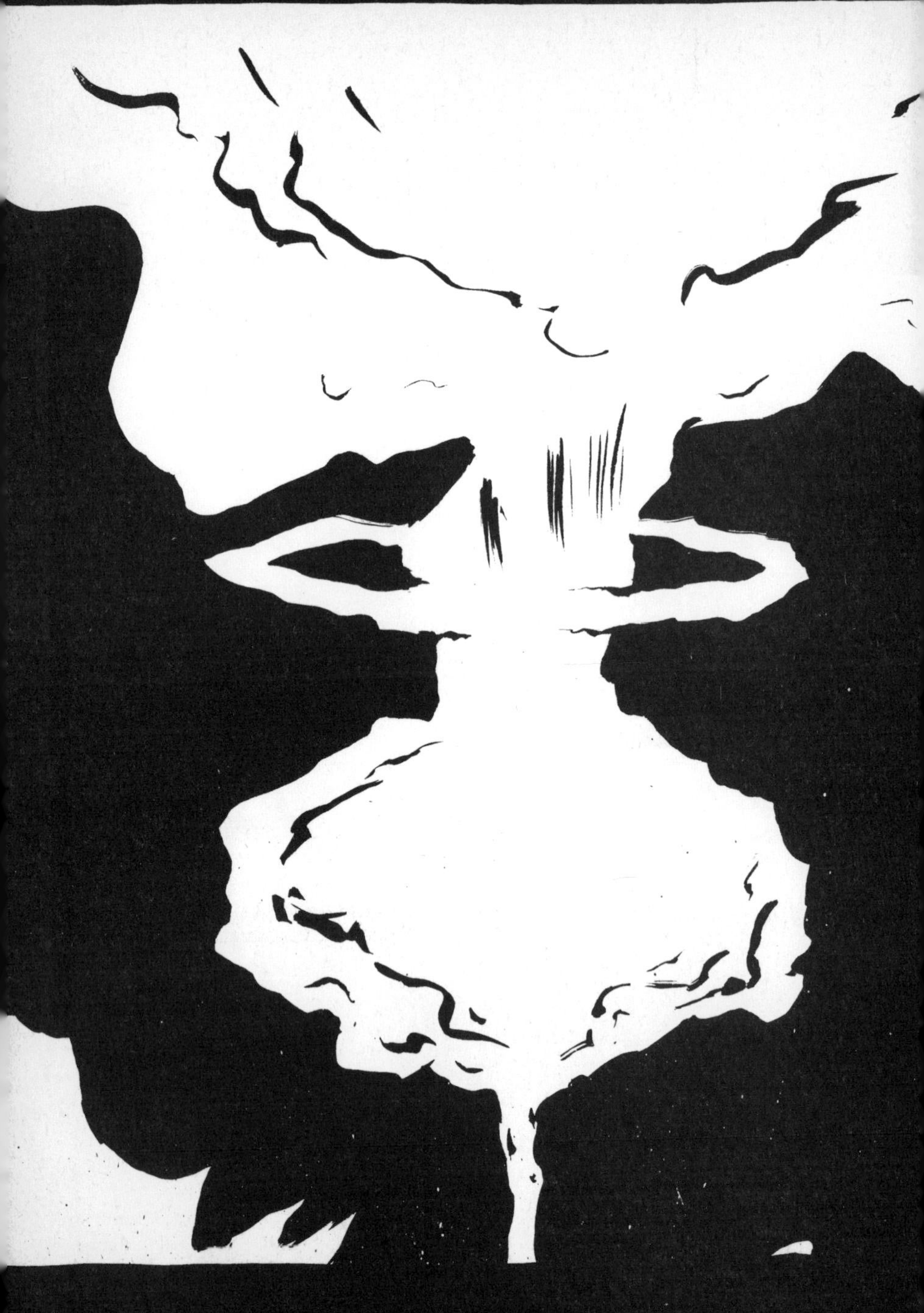

EPILOGUE.

THIRTY YEARS LATER...

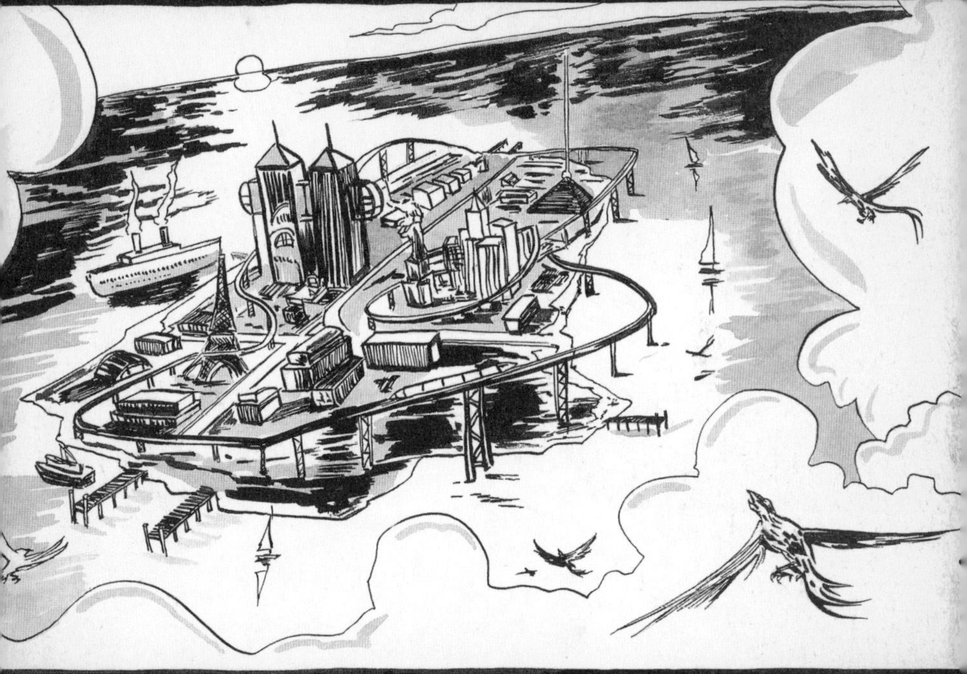

NEW LAS VEGAS ISLAND.

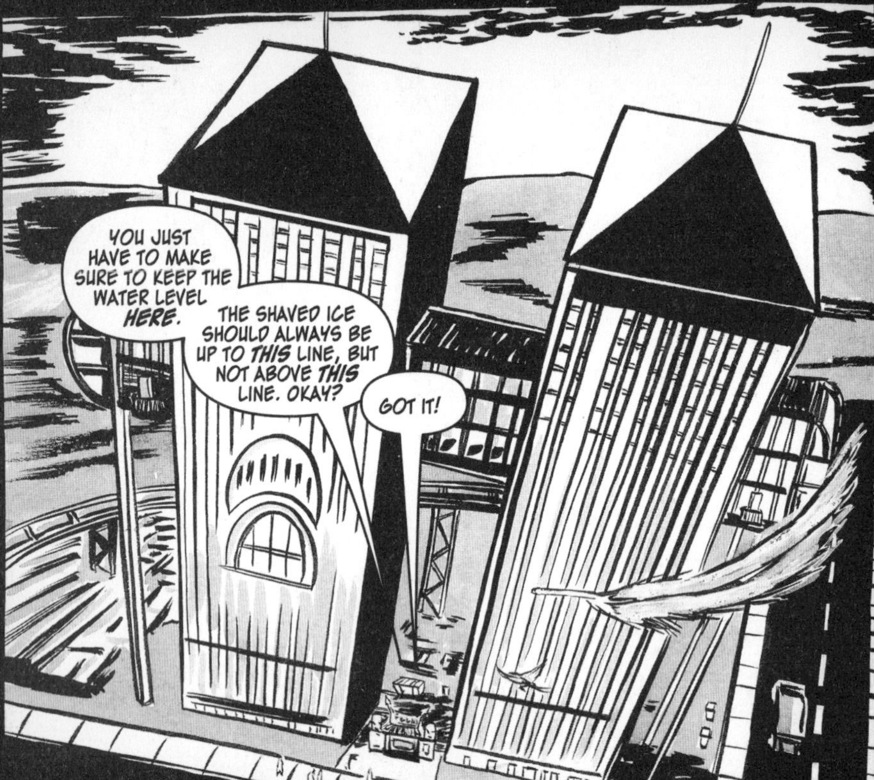
YOU JUST HAVE TO MAKE SURE TO KEEP THE WATER LEVEL *HERE*.
THE SHAVED ICE SHOULD ALWAYS BE UP TO *THIS* LINE, BUT NOT ABOVE *THIS* LINE. OKAY?
GOT IT!

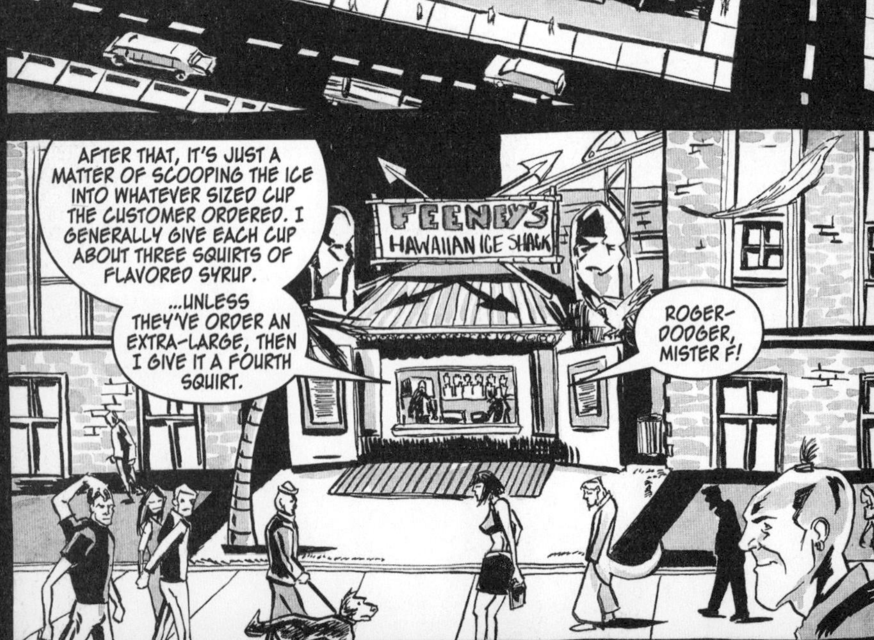
AFTER THAT, IT'S JUST A MATTER OF SCOOPING THE ICE INTO WHATEVER SIZED CUP THE CUSTOMER ORDERED. I GENERALLY GIVE EACH CUP ABOUT THREE SQUIRTS OF FLAVORED SYRUP.
FEENEY'S
HAWAIIAN ICE SHACK
...UNLESS THEY'VE ORDER AN EXTRA-LARGE, THEN I GIVE IT A FOURTH SQUIRT.
ROGER-DODGER, MISTER F!

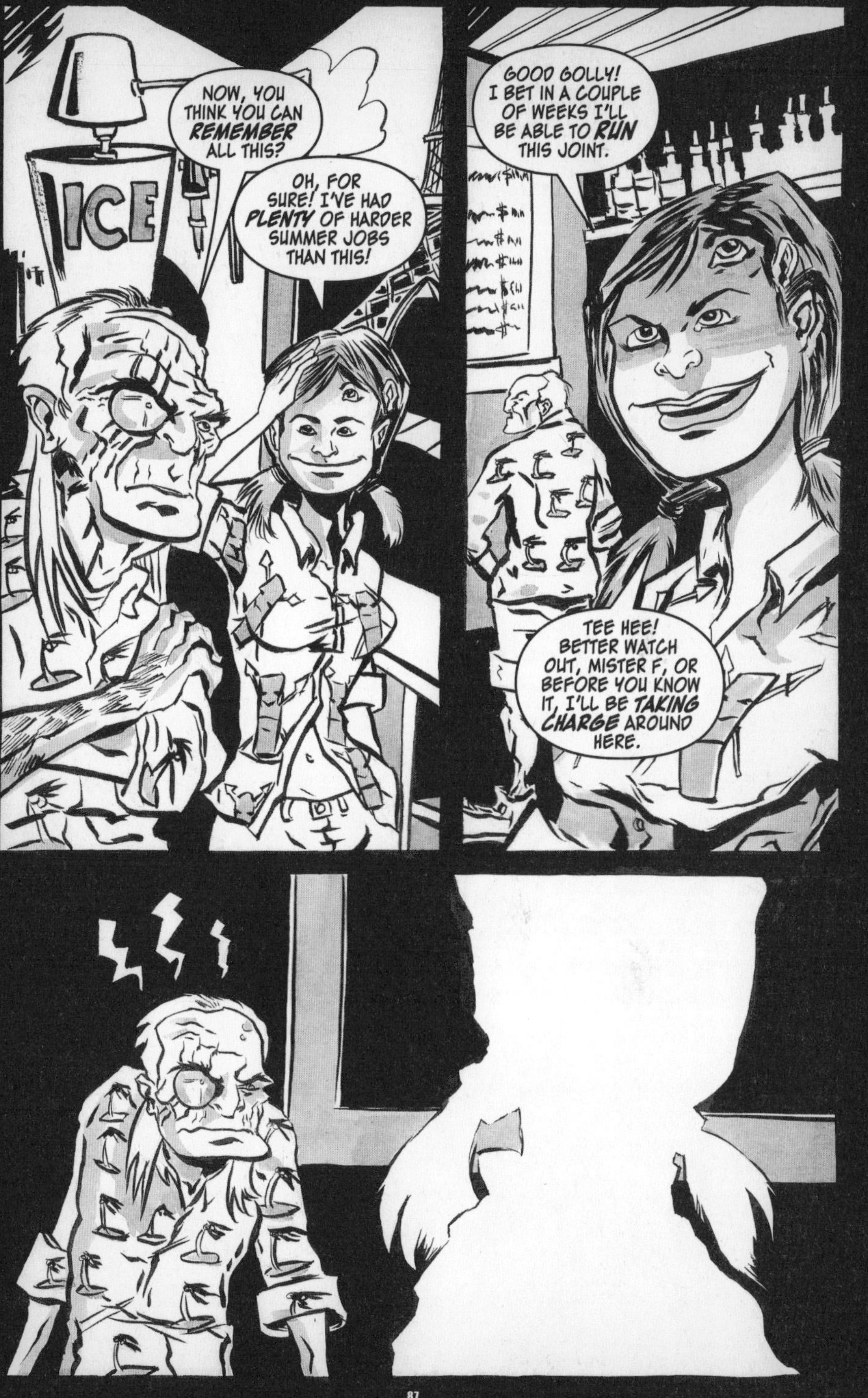
NOW, YOU THINK YOU CAN REMEMBER ALL THIS?
OH, FOR SURE! I'VE HAD PLENTY OF HARDER SUMMER JOBS THAN THIS!
ICE
GOOD GOLLY! I BET IN A COUPLE OF WEEKS I'LL BE ABLE TO RUN THIS JOINT.
TEE HEE! BETTER WATCH OUT, MISTER F, OR BEFORE YOU KNOW IT, I'LL BE TAKING CHARGE AROUND HERE.

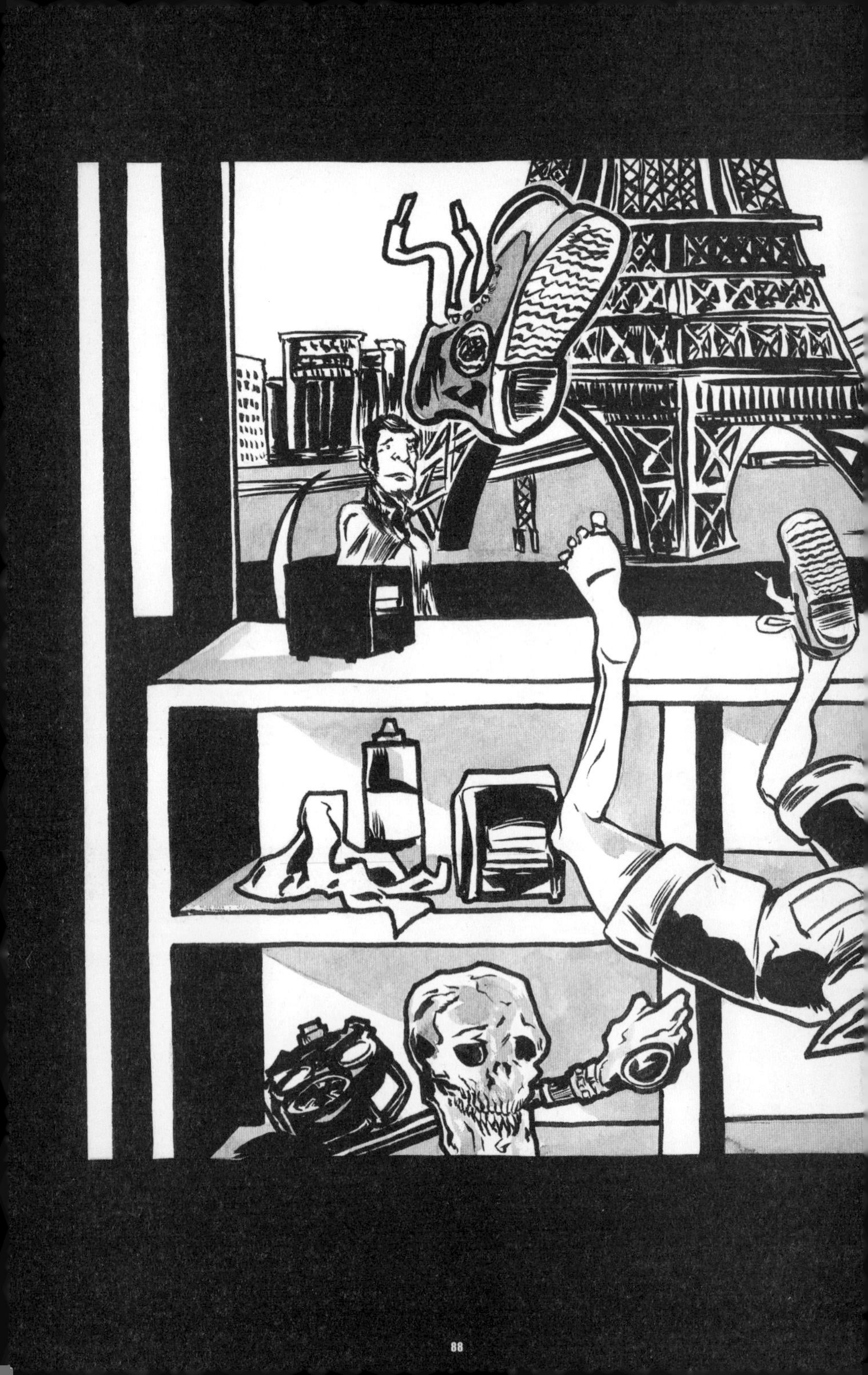

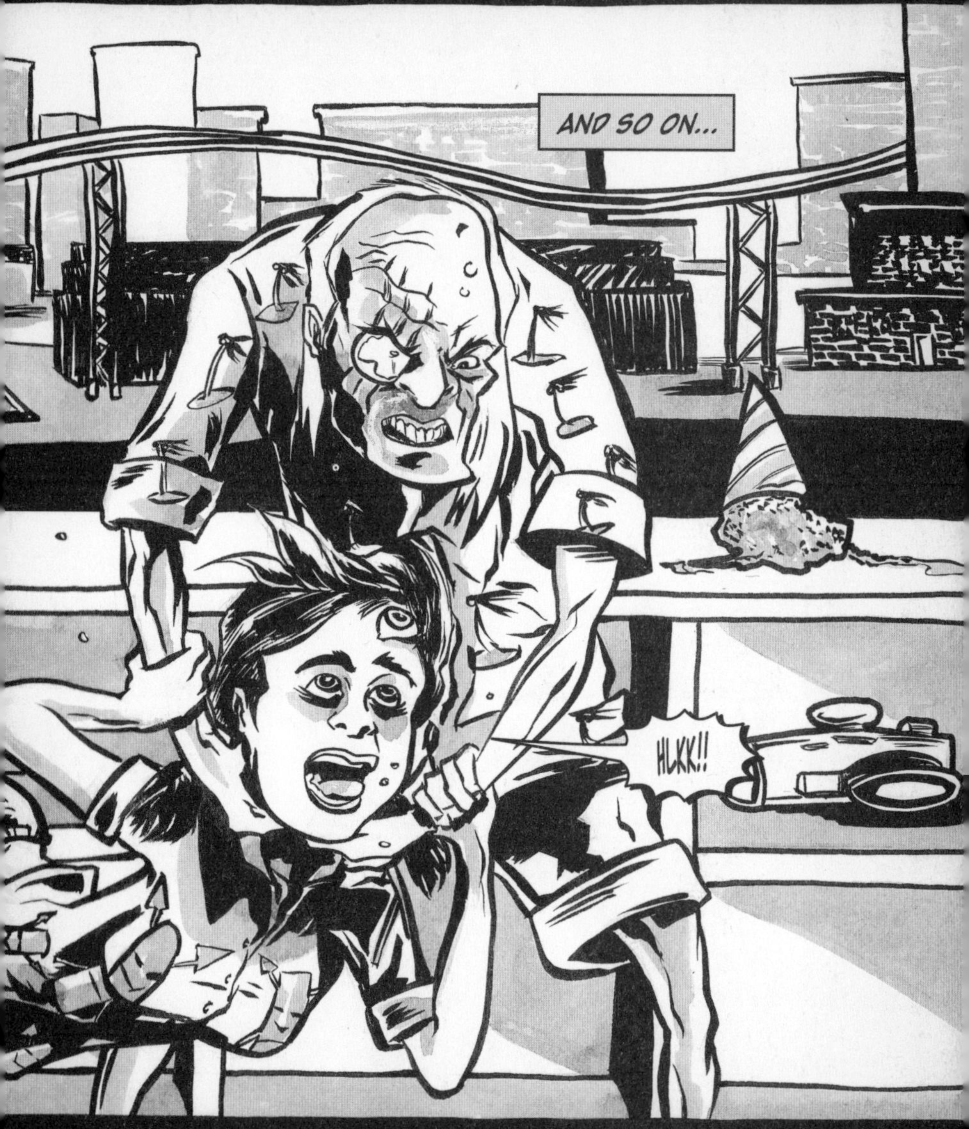
AND SO ON...
HLKK!!

THE END.

# JOHN LAYMAN

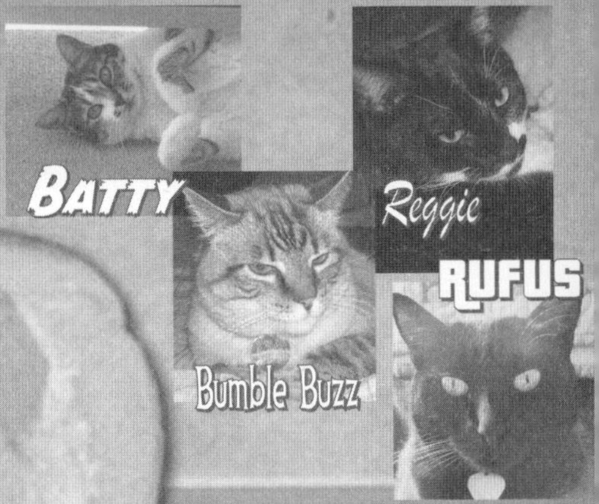

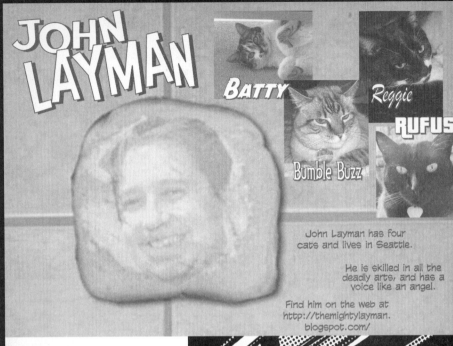

Batty
Reggie
Rufus
Bumble Buzz


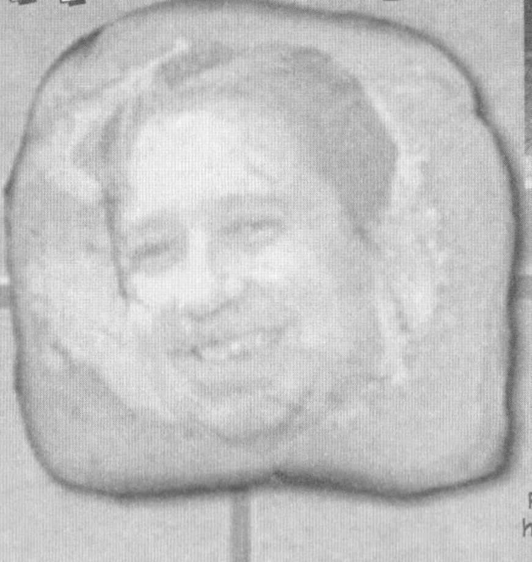

John Layman has four cats and lives in Seattle.

He is skilled in all the deadly arts, and has a voice like an angel.

Find him on the web at http://themightylayman.blogspot.com/

***DAVID DUMEER*** IS A FREELANCE ARTIST WHO HAS BEEN CONFINED TO A DAMP DARK ROOM FOR THE LAST SEVEN YEARS WHERE ALL PURITY HAS BEEN DRAINED FROM HIS PRECIOUS BODILY FLUIDS. CURRENTLY, DAVID LIVES IN THE WESTERN MOUNTAINS OF VIRGINIA AND WHEN HE IS NOT PLANTED BEHIND HIS DRAWING TABLE, HE ENJOYS SPENDING TIME WITH HIS BEAUTIFUL WIFE.

TO LEARN MORE ABOUT THIS SADLY DEPRAVED INDIVIDUAL VISIT HIM AT:

***WWW.DUMEER.COM***

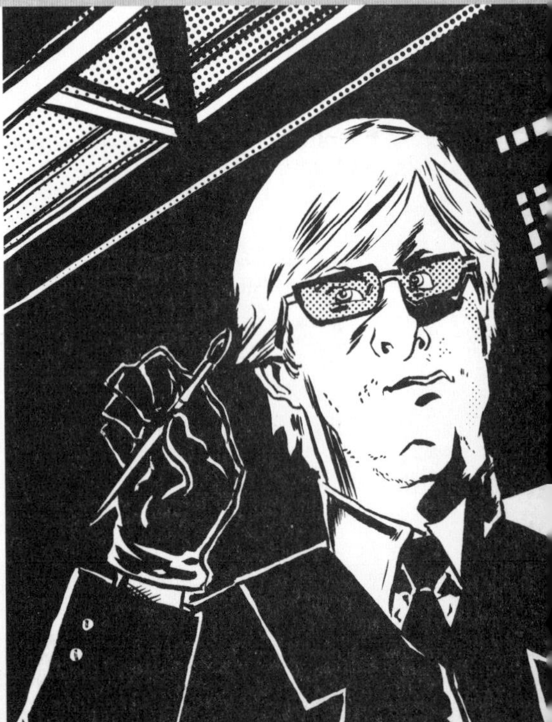

# AFTERWORD

This book was written in Seattle during a period when my father was having severe health problems and I was spending far too much of my time watching spy movies. It's pretty easy to see that the story was a weird amalgamation of both.

It has since gone through various incarnations. Originally titled "Feeney" and conceived as a three part mini, it was later re-dubbed "F-Bomb," which I thought was a more marketable title. I also decided to go the OGN route, because I wasn't sure the humor would show through as well in separate chunks as it would as a unified whole.

I met Dave Dumeer online at this time, trolling various comic book artist message boards and online hangouts like a lonely, desperate sailor. I was immediately enamored with his stuff, and he did ten sample pages for us to pitch. The rest, as they say, is history.

After it was picked up by Oni, it was finally re-titled "Armageddon & Son," so it would not be confused with Oni's other fine-graphic novel, "F-Stop." We also decided on the format, and were able to let the story breathe a little better with added space and extra scenes (so it's sorta like you seeing the directors cut without ever reading the original.)

Thanks to Dave Dumeer, for his patience and for being such a great collaborator. Thanks to James Lucas Jones, Joe Nozemack, Maryanne Snell, and especially Randal C. Jarrell for believing in the project, supporting it, and supplying their expert input and feedback. Thanks to Mike Heisler and Tom Peyer for editorial advice and suggestions.

And, of course, thanks to you, for picking the book up and giving it a shot. You're swell.

- JLayman
8/30/05

# OTHER BOOKS FROM ONI PRESS...

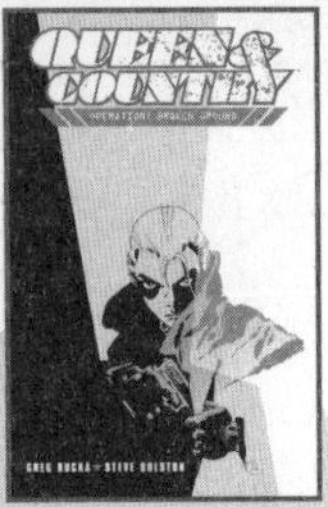

QUEEN & COUNTRY


QUEEN & COUNTRY, VOL. 1:
OPERATION: BROKEN GROUND™
By Greg Rucka & Steve Rolston
128 Pages, black-and-white interiors
$11.95 us
ISBN 1-929998-21-X

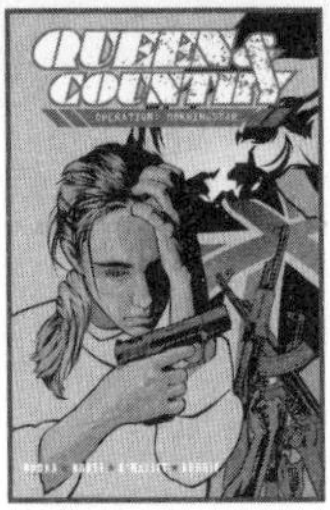

QUEEN & COUNTRY


QUEEN & COUNTRY, VOL. 2:
OPERATION: MORNING STAR™
By Greg Rucka & Brian Hurtt
88 Pages, black-and-white interiors
$8.95 us
ISBN 1-929998-35-X

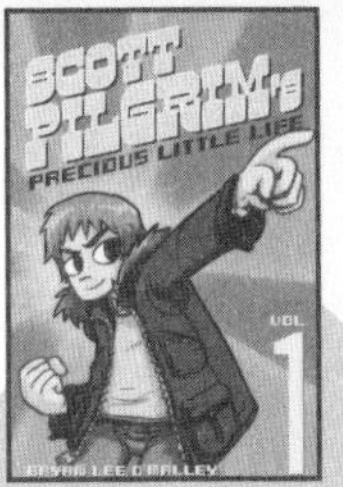

SCOTT PILGRIM'S
PRECIOUS LITTLE LIFE
VOL 1
BRYAN LEE O'MALLEY


SCOTT PILGRIM™, VOL. 1:
SCOTT PILGRIM'S PRECIOUS LITTLE LIFE
By Bryan Lee O'Malley
168 Pages, black-and-white interiors
$11.95 us
ISBN 1-932664-08-4

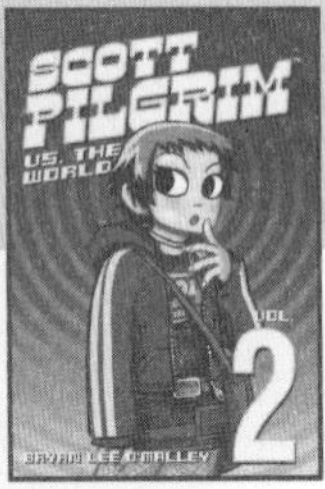

SCOTT PILGRIM
VS. THE WORLD
VOL. 2
BRYAN LEE O'MALLEY


SCOTT PILGRIM™, VOL. 2:
SCOTT PILGRIM VS. THE WORLD
By Bryan Lee O'Malley
200 Pages, black-and-white interiors
$11.95 us
ISBN 1-932664-12-2

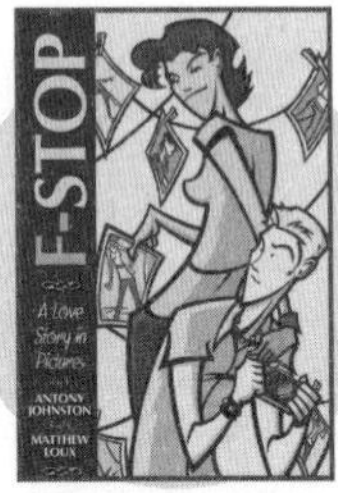

F-STOP
A Love Story in Pictures
ANTONY JOHNSTON
MATTHEW LOUX


F-STOP™
By Antony Johnston & Matthew Loux
168 Pages, black-and-white interiors
$14.95 us
ISBN 1-932664-09-2

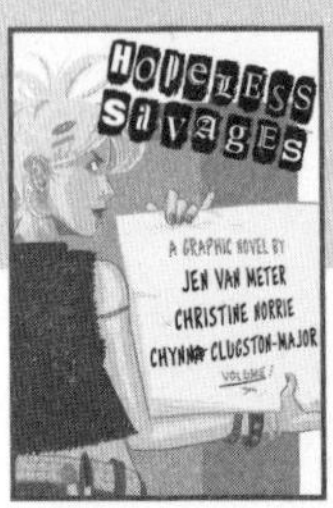

HOPELESS SAVAGES
A GRAPHIC NOVEL BY
JEN VAN METER
CHRISTINE NORRIE
CHYNNA CLUGSTON-MAJOR


Hopeless Savages, Vol. 1TM
By Jen Van Meter, Christine Norrie,
& Chynna Clugston-Major
136 pages, black-and-white interiors
$11.95 US
ISBN 1-929998-75-9

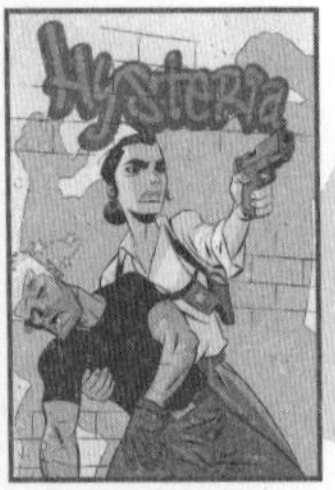

Hysteria


HYSTERIA™
By Mike Hawthorne
104 Pages, black-and-white interiors
$9.95 us
ISBN 1-929998-90-2

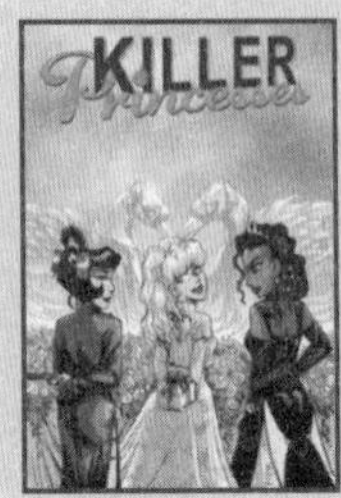

KILLER
Princesses


KILLER PRINCESSES™
By Gail Simone & Lea Hernandez
96 Pages, black-and-white interiors
$9.95 us
ISBN 1929998-31-7

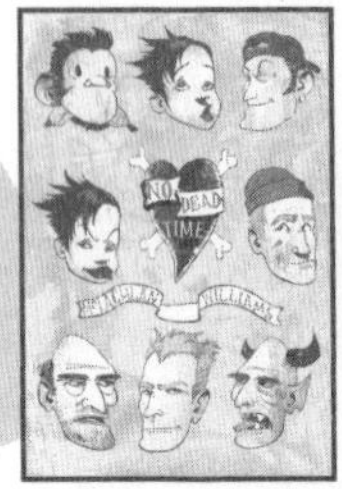

NO DEAD TIME™
By Brian McLachlan & Thomas Williams
136 Pages, black-and-white interiors
$12.95 us
ISBN 1-932664-02-5

Available at finer comics shops everywhere. For a comics store near you, call 1-888-COMIC-BOOK or visit www.the-master-list.com. For more Oni Press titles and information visit www.onipress.com.